CW01665430

Earth and Space

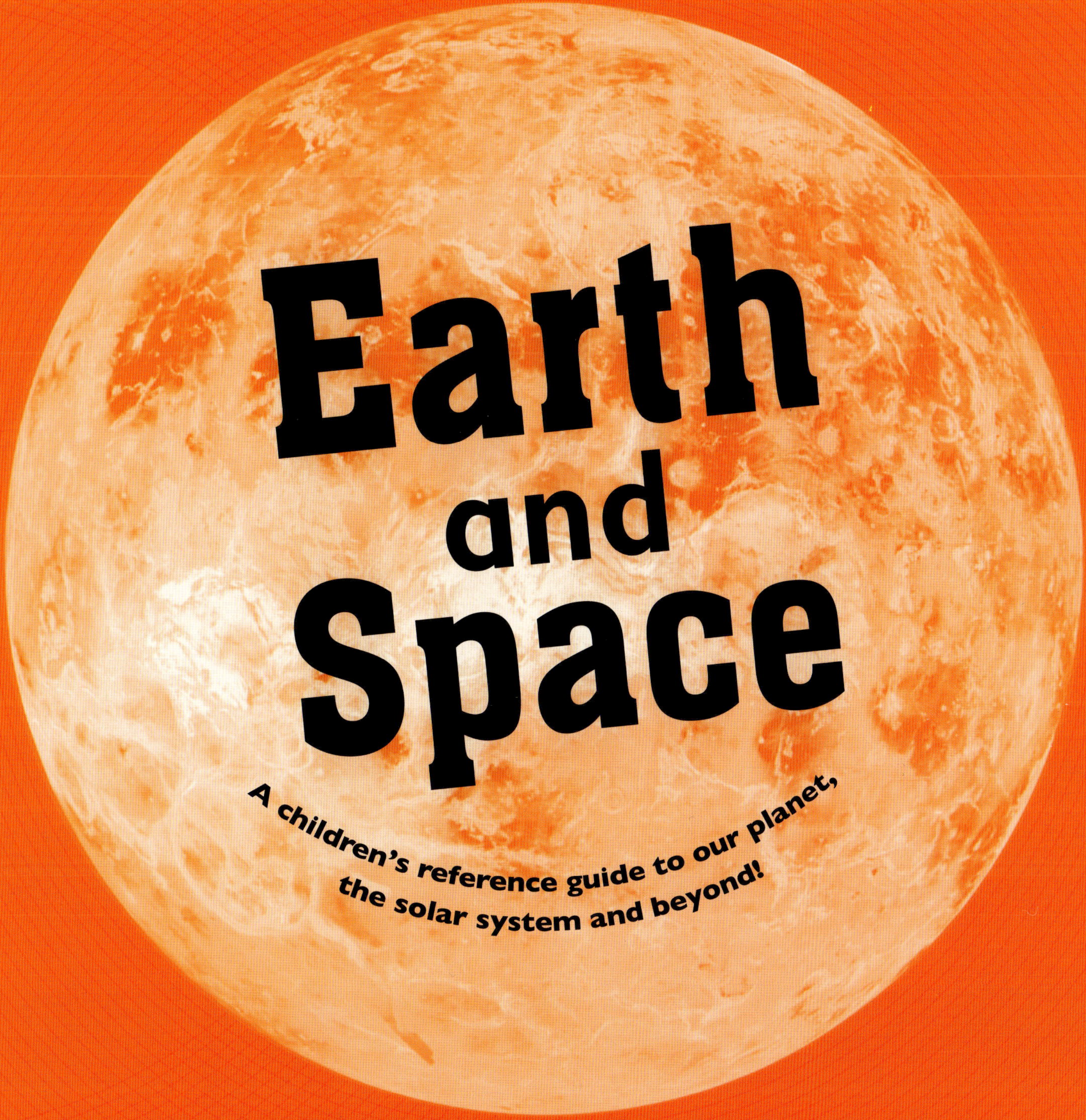

A children's reference guide to our planet, the solar system and beyond!

Written by: Anita Ganeri, John Malam,
Clare Oliver, Adam Hibbert

Cover images:
Front: t Getty Images, m Getty Images, b Getty Images
Back: t iStockphoto.com, tr iStockphoto.com, mr iStockphoto.com, br Getty Images

This edition published by Parragon in 2012
Parragon
Queen Street House
4 Queen Street
Bath BA1 1HE, UK
www.parragon.com

Copyright © Parragon Books Ltd 2001

Originally produced by David West Children's Books
This edition by Design Principals

Illustrators John Butler Jim Eldridge James Field Andrew & Angela Harland
Colin Howard Rob Jakeway Mike Lacey Sarah Lees Gilly Marklew Dud Moseley
Terry Riley Sarah Smith Stephen Sweet Mike Taylor Ross Watton (SGA) Ian Thompson
Cartoonist Peter Wilks (SGA)
Editor James Pickering Consultant Steve Parker

All rights reserved. No part of this publication may be reproduced, stored in a retrieval system or transmitted, in any form or by any means, electronic, mechanical, photocopying, recording or otherwise, without the prior permission of the copyright holder.

British Library Cataloguing-in-Publication Data
A catalogue record for this book is available from the British Library.

ISBN 978-1-78186-071-7

Printed in China

iknow stuff

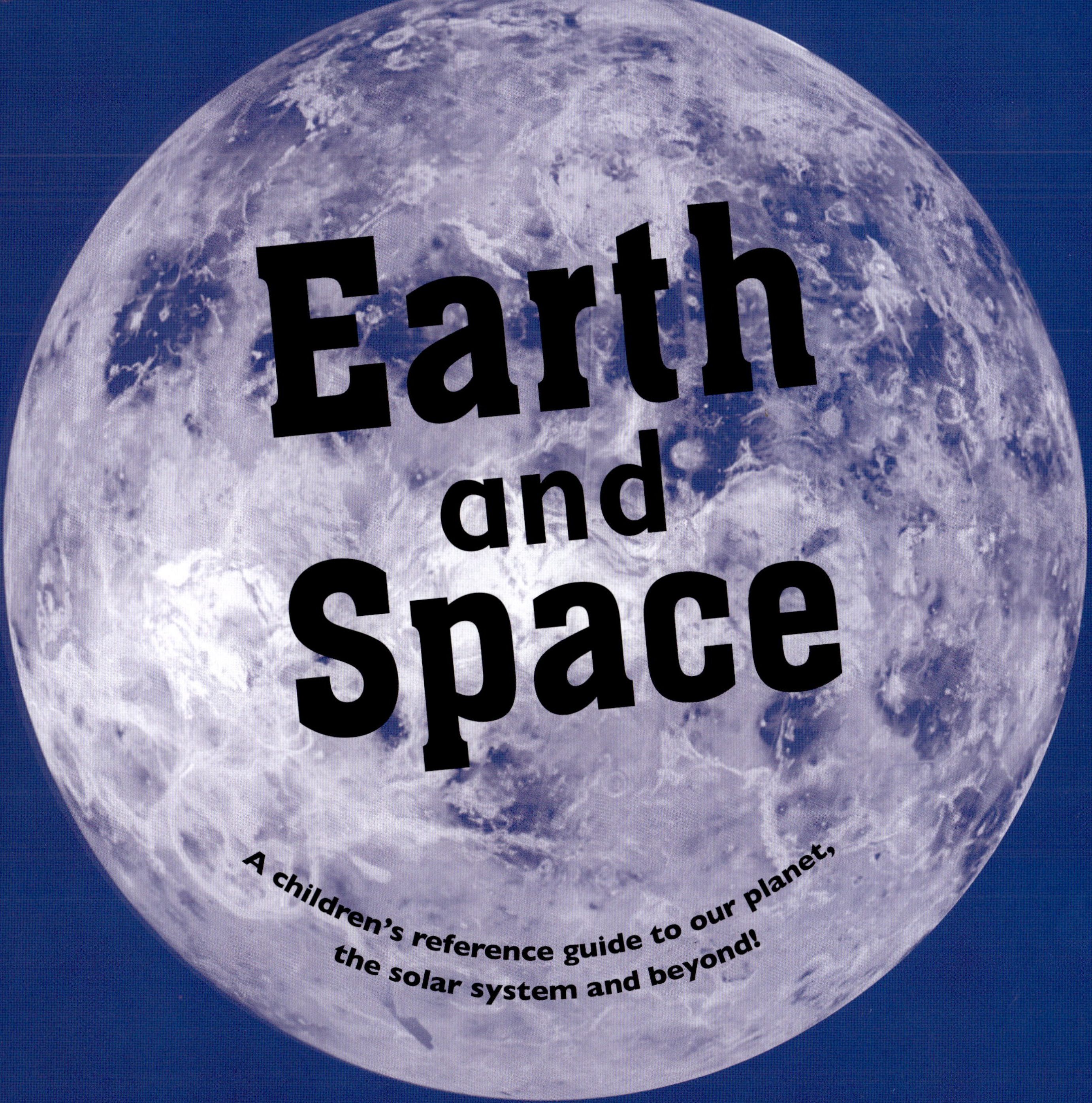

Earth and Space

A children's reference guide to our planet, the solar system and beyond!

Parragon

Bath • New York • Singapore • Hong Kong • Cologne • Delhi
Melbourne • Amsterdam • Johannesburg • Shenzhen

Contents

CHAPTER ONE
OUR SOLAR SYSTEM

CHAPTER TWO
SPACE EXPLORATION

CHAPTER THREE
BEYOND OUR SOLAR SYSTEM

CHAPTER FIVE
PREHISTORIC LIFE ON EARTH

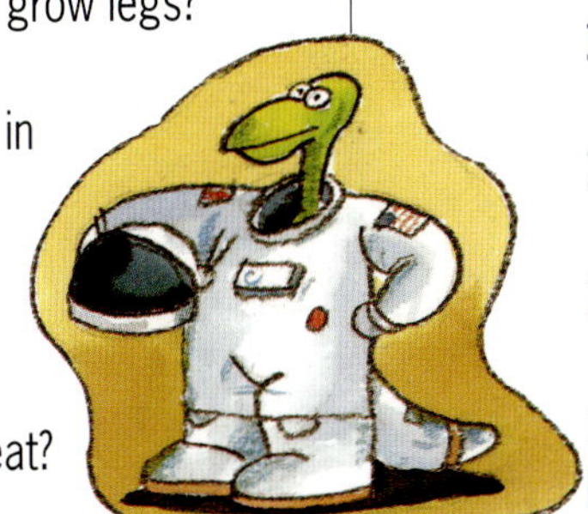

CHAPTER SIX
EXPLORING EARTH

CHAPTER SEVEN
VIOLENT EARTH

CHAPTER ONE

OUR SOLAR SYSTEM

What is the Solar System?

Solar means 'of the Sun'. The Solar System is centred around the Sun, the shining ball in the sky. It includes the family of eight planets orbiting (travelling around) the Sun, as well as the moons of these planets and smaller objects, such as comets, asteroids and bits of space rock. The powerful pull of an invisible force called gravity from the Sun stops these bodies from flying off into deepest space.

Uranus

Distance from Sun
2,870 million km
Diameter
51,118 km

Neptune

Distance from Sun
4,497 million km
Diameter
49,532 km

Is it true?

All planets have one moon.

NO. Our planet Earth has one moon, called the Moon. But many of the planets have more than one. Our neighbour Mars, for instance, has two! Only the two planets closest to the Sun – Mercury and Venus – have no moons at all.

Amazing! Saturn's not the only planet with rings. Saturn's rings are the easiest to see, but Jupiter, Neptune and Uranus have them, too. Saturn has seven main rings, and then hundreds of thinner rings, called ringlets.

How hot is the Sun?

In deserts here on Earth, heat that has travelled 150 million km from the Sun can be hot enough to fry an egg. The Sun's surface is a super-hot 6,000°C, and its centre or core is even hotter.

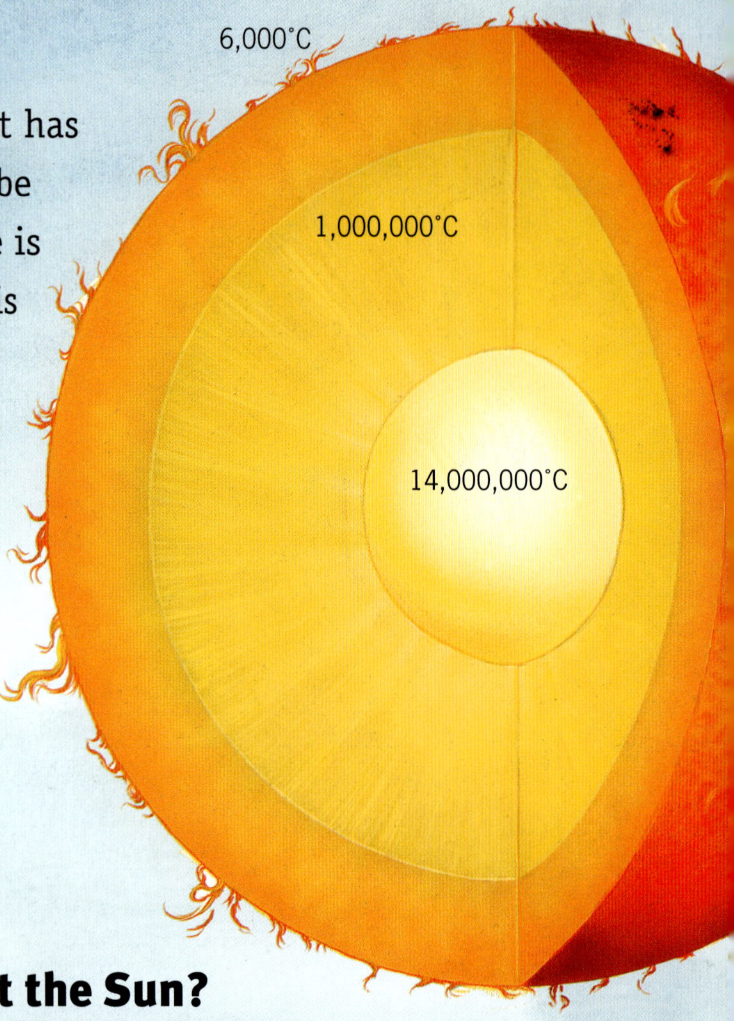

Amazing!
The Sun is a star – a gigantic ball of burning gas. It has been shining for about five billion years.

Why must you never look at the Sun?

Not even sunglasses fully protect your eyes from the Sun's dangerous ultraviolet (UV) rays. UV can burn your eyes and make you blind. If you want to see the Sun safely, ask an adult to show you how to project its image on to a sheet of paper.

Is it true?

The Sun has spots.

YES. The Sun is not the same colour all over. Some areas of its surface are darker. These spots are little pockets that are slightly cooler. Of course, sunspots are only 'little' compared to the Sun – some grow to be as large as Jupiter, the biggest planet in the Solar System!

Total eclipse of the Sun

When does the Sun go out?

When there's a total eclipse. This happens when the Moon's path takes it between the Earth and the Sun, and the Moon casts a shadow across the surface of the Earth.

What does Mercury look like?

Planet Mercury looks very like our Moon. It's about the same size and it's covered in craters, where bits of space rock have crash-landed on its surface. The biggest crater is the Caloris Basin, which is about 1,300 km across. Mercury also has huge plains, rolling hills, deep gorges, chasms and cliffs.

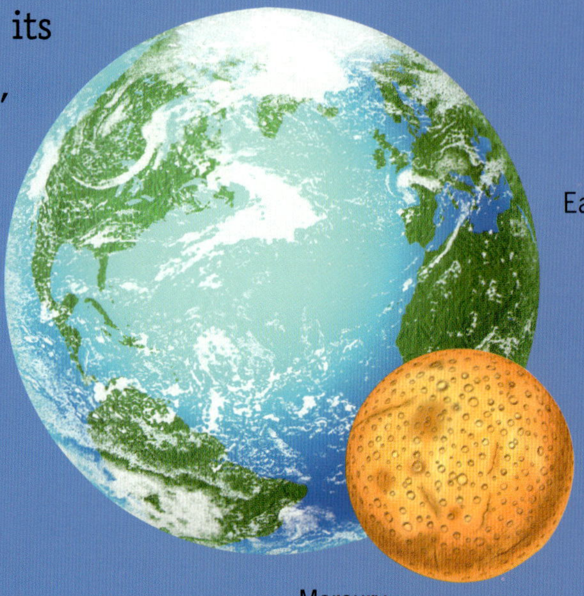

The surface of Mercury is covered with craters

Is it true?

Mercury is the smallest planet.

YES. Mercury is now the smallest planet and is only about a third the size of Earth. The smallest planet used to be Pluto, but Pluto was declared a dwarf planet in 2006.

Is Mercury the hottest planet?

Mercury is the planet closest to the Sun, but its neighbour Venus is even hotter, because it has clouds to keep in the heat.

The surface of Mercury is 350°C during the day, and minus 170°C at night

What is the weather like on Mercury?

Mercury doesn't have any weather, because it has no air and hardly any atmosphere. That means there are no clouds to shield the surface of the planet from the baking-hot Sun during the day, or to keep in the heat at night. There is no wind or rain on Mercury, either.

Amazing! Mercury is the fastest planet. Mercury zooms around the Sun in just 88 days, at an incredible 173,000 kph. That makes it faster than any space rocket ever invented.

The planet Venus seen close to the Moon

When is a star not a star?

When it's a planet! Venus is sometimes called the 'evening star' because it's so bright it's one of the first points of light we see shining as it gets dark. Planets don't make their own light – they reflect the Sun's light.

Is it true?

Venus is bigger than the Earth.

NO. Venus is a fraction smaller than the Earth, but not by much. Venus is about 12,104 km across, whereas Earth is about 650 km wider. Venus's mass is about four-fifths of Earth's.

How can a day be longer than a year?

A day is the amount of time a planet takes to spin on its axis, and a year is the time it takes to travel around the Sun. Venus spins on its axis very slowly, but orbits the Sun more quickly than Earth. A day on Venus lasts 243 Earth-days, but a year is only 225 Earth-days.

Volcanic eruption on Venus

Amazing!

Venus is named after a goddess. Venus was the name of the Roman goddess of love and beauty – just right for the planet, which many people think is the most beautiful object in the sky.

What's special about our planet?

As far as we know, Earth is the only planet in the Solar System that has life. As well as warmth from the Sun, the other main ingredient for life is liquid water. Earth has plenty of water – in total, it covers about three-quarters of the planet's surface!

Earth seen from space

Is it true?

There was life on Earth from the start.

NO. When Earth first formed it was extremely hot and there was no oxygen. Over millions of years, the planet cooled, oceans formed and oxygen was made. The first life on Earth appeared about 3 billion years ago.

What does Earth look like from space?

It looks beautiful – blue with swirling white clouds. Astronauts in space spend most of their free time gazing at it. They can even make out cities, when they are lit up at night with twinkling lights.

Amazing!

The Earth is magnetic. At the centre of the Earth is a core of a molten metal called iron, which makes our planet like a giant magnet. This is what pulls the needle on a compass towards the magnetic North Pole.

Why does our sky go dark at night?

Like all planets, the Earth is spinning as it orbits the Sun. When your part of the planet is facing away from the Sun, its light is blocked out. At the same time, it is daytime for people on the opposite side of the Earth.

New Moon Crescent Moon First quarter Moon Gibbous Moon

Why does the Moon change shape?

It doesn't really – it's ball-shaped just like the Earth, but as the Moon travels around the Earth, you see different amounts of its sunlit half. It seems to change gradually from a crescent to a disc, and back again.

Why does the Moon have so many craters?

Because it has been pelted by so many space rocks and has no atmosphere to protect it. One of the biggest craters, called Bailly, is nearly 300 km across. You can make out some of the craters using a good pair of binoculars.

Meteorite hitting the Moon

What is the dark side of the Moon?

It's the part of the Moon that we can never see from Earth. The Moon takes the same time to orbit the Earth as it does to spin once. This means the same side of the Moon always faces away from the Earth.

Full Moon

Amazing! You can jump higher on the Moon. The Moon's gravity is much weaker than Earth's. This means you would only weigh about a sixth of your Earth-weight there – and you'd be able to jump six times higher!

Is it true?

There are seas on the Moon.

YES AND NO. There are dark, rocky plains and craters called maria (from the Latin for 'sea'), but they don't contain water. The first astronauts to visit the Moon landed on the Sea of Tranquillity.

One of Mars's polar caps, at the bottom of the planet

Does Mars have ice at its poles?

Yes. Its south pole is mostly 'dry ice', which is frozen carbon dioxide gas. At the north pole there may be frozen water, mixed with the frozen carbon dioxide. There may be frozen water underground on Mars, too.

Earth

Mars

Which is the red planet?

Mars was named after the Roman god of war, because of its blood-red colour. The planet looks rusty red because its surface is covered with iron-rich soil and rock. There are no seas on Mars, and it is very cold.

The Martian surface, showing Olympus Mons

Is it true?

There is life on Mars.

NO. Or at least, there's no sure sign of any. But long ago, Mars had flowing rivers of water, so there could have been life once, and there may be fossils buried underground.

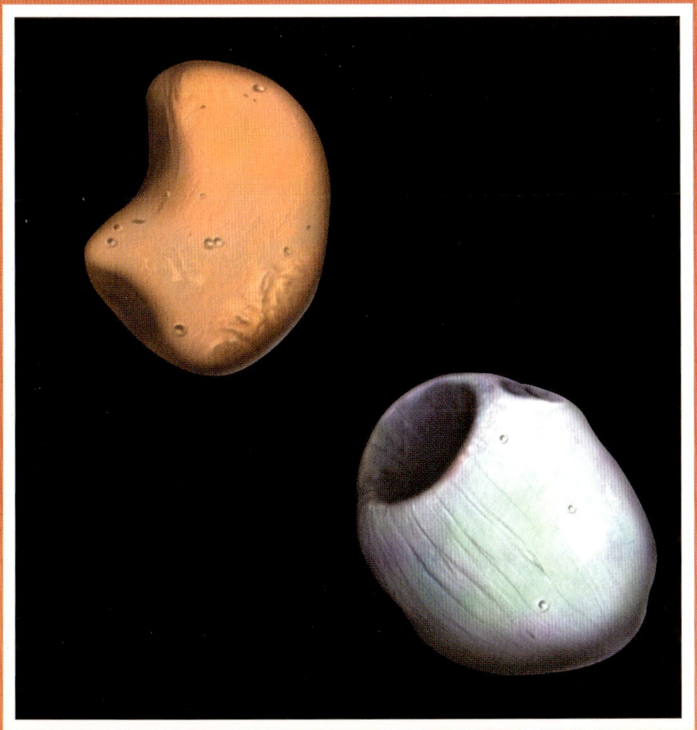

Phobos
(about 15 km long)

Deimos
(about 27 km long)

What are Mars's moons like?

Mars's two tiny moons, Deimos and Phobos, are not round like our Moon. They look more like baked potatoes! They might have been asteroids (space rocks) that Mars captured with its gravity.

Amazing! There's a record-breaking volcano on Mars. Olympus Mons is about 600 km across and towers over 25 km high. It's the Solar System's biggest volcano. Long ago it spurted out runny rivers of black lava.

Which is the biggest planet?

Jupiter is so big that all the other planets in the Solar System could fit inside it! If it was any bigger it might become too hot in the middle, start to glow and turn into another Sun.

Is it true?

Jupiter's stripy.

YES. The planet looks like it's wearing a giant pair of pyjamas, because of its bands of cloud. They're made of frozen crystals of water, ammonia and other chemicals.

What is Jupiter made of?

Jupiter is one of the planets known as the gas giants. About 90 per cent of it is made of gases called hydrogen and helium. At the centre of Jupiter is a small, rocky core, about as big as the Earth.

Amazing! You could fit two Earths inside the Great Red Spot, which is about 40,000 km across.

Where is the storm that never stops?

Violent winds whip up storms all over the planet Jupiter, but the Great Red Spot is the largest. It has been raging away for over 300 years!

The Great Red Spot is a giant storm on Jupiter

Looking at Jupiter from Io

Which world has most volcanoes?

Jupiter's closest moon, Io, is orange and yellow, because of the sulphur from all its active volcanoes. If you could survive the intense heat, you'd realize that Io smells of rotten eggs!

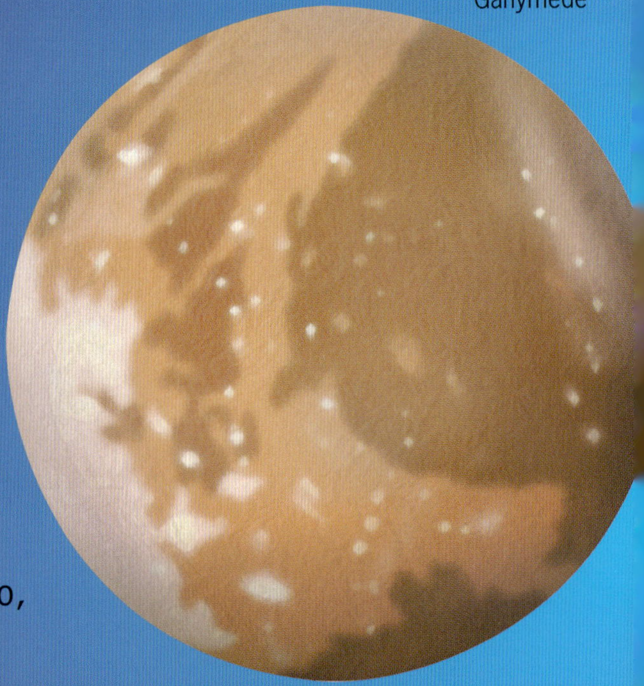

Ganymede

Which moon is bigger than a planet?

Jupiter's moon Ganymede is the largest moon in the Solar System. At 5,276 km across, it is bigger than Mercury! Another of Jupiter's moons, Callisto, is a similar size to Mercury.

Looking at Jupiter from Ganymede

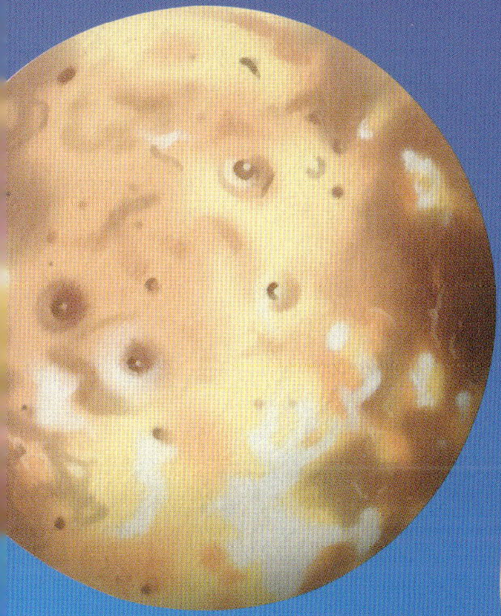

Which moon might have life?

Jupiter's moon Europa is covered by a thick crust of ice. The ice looks smooth, like frozen water, but it also has lots of cracks. Scientists think there is a liquid ocean beneath the ice – and where there's water, there might be life!

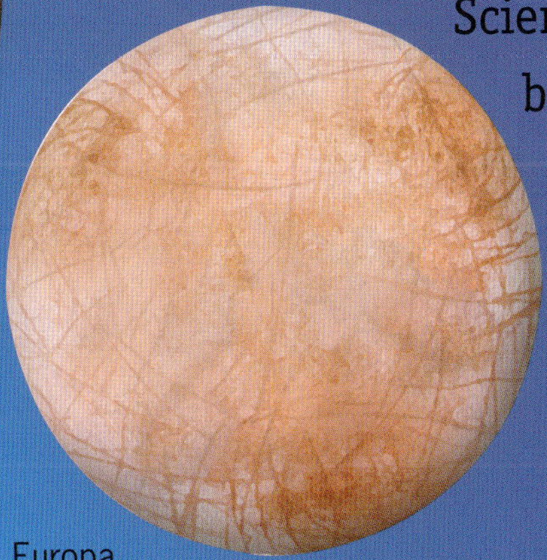

Europa

Amazing! Callisto is the most cratered world in the Solar System. Almost every bit of this moon is covered in craters. The biggest one is about 300 km across. It is called Valhalla, after the place where the Vikings thought brave warriors went when they died.

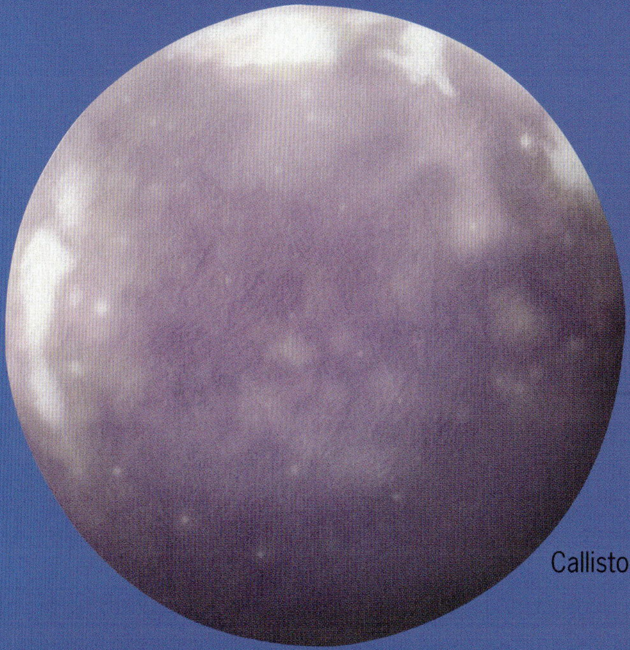

Callisto

Is it true?
Jupiter only has four moons.

NO. Galileo discovered the four biggest – Callisto, Ganymede, Europa and Io – in 1610. Since then astronomers have discovered even more moons, making a total of 63!

Saturn's rings viewed from its upper atmosphere

Amazing! You could fit about 740 Earths into Saturn. It is the Solar System's second largest planet, after Jupiter. Its rings are 270,000 km across – about twice the width of the planet.

Are Saturn's rings solid?

No – they look solid, but they are made up of millions of chunks of ice and rock. The smallest chunks are about the size of a golf ball, while the biggest are about a kilometre wide.

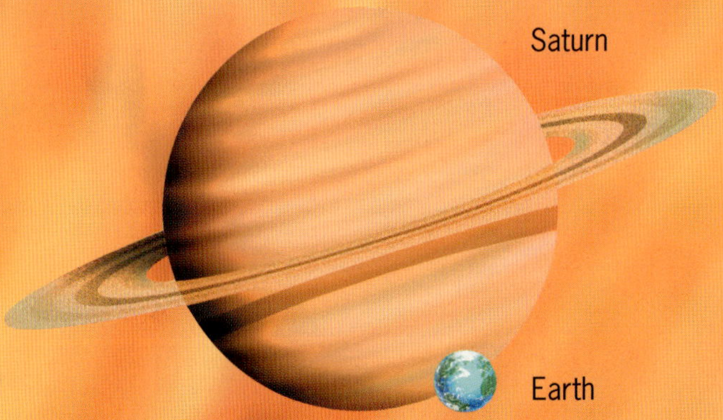

Saturn viewed from above Titan

Do Saturn's rings have names?

Not really, but scientists have given each ring a letter so that they know which one they are talking about. There are seven main rings, of which the three brightest are A, B and C.

How many moons does Saturn have?

Saturn has at least 18 moons, but there may be more. The biggest is Titan – the second largest moon in the Solar System. Titan is covered by clouds, so we can't see its surface.

Is it true?

Saturn is light enough to float.

YES. Saturn is made up of liquid and gas, with a small rocky centre. It is so light that, if there was an ocean big enough, the planet would float on it like a boat!

William Herschel

Which planet was found by accident?

Uranus was discovered in 1781. The man who found it, William Herschel, was not expecting to find a planet at all. He thought he was pointing his homemade telescope at a distant star.

How many moons does Uranus have?

Uranus has at least 17 moons – but there could be more to discover. They are all named after characters from English literature. The main ones are Oberon, Titania, Umbriel, Ariel and Miranda. Ophelia and Cordelia are the closest.

Amazing! The poles on Uranus are warmer than the equator. Because Uranus is tilted on its side, the poles are the warmest places on the planet. Summer at the south pole lasts 42 years!

Miranda

Approaching Uranus through its rings

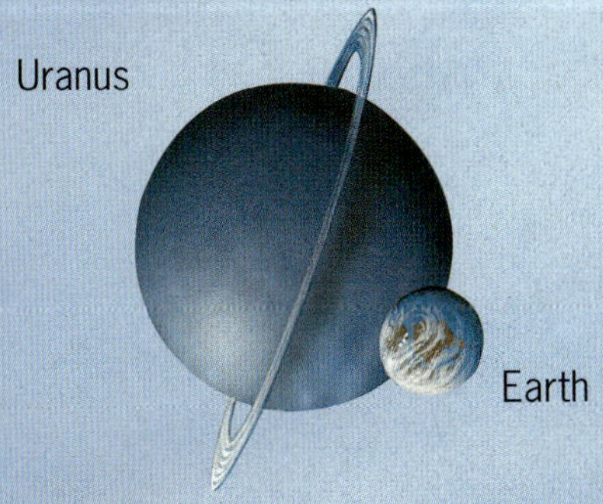

Why is Uranus blue?

The bluish-green is the colour of methane, a stinky gas that makes up part of Uranus's atmosphere. The other gases in the air there are hydrogen and helium – the gas we use to fill party balloons.

Is it true?

Uranus was nearly called George.

YES. When Herschel discovered the new planet, he wanted to name it after the English king at the time, George III. In the end, it was called Uranus, after the Greek god of the sky.

Which planet has pulling power?

Astronomers knew Neptune must be there before they saw it! They could tell something big was pulling Uranus and they were able to predict exactly where Neptune was – almost 4.5 billion kilometres away from the Sun.

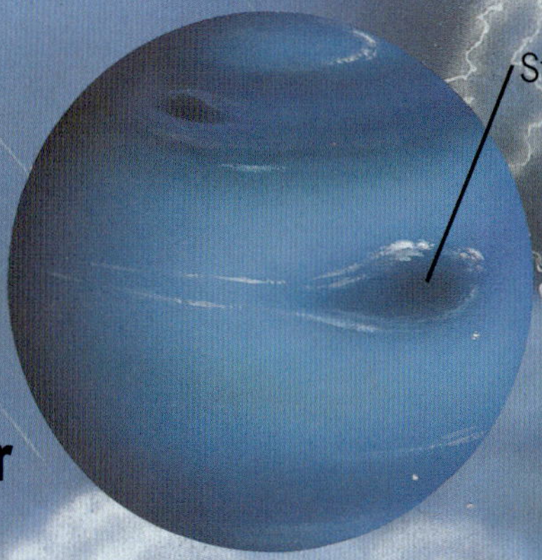

Storm on Neptune

What's the weather like on Neptune?

Very, very windy! Winds rip across the planet all the time, much faster than any winds on Earth. There are also lots of storms on Neptune, which show up as dark spots. This means Neptune's appearance is constantly changing.

Amazing! **Triton is one of the coldest places ever recorded! The temperature on the ice-covered moon is minus 236°C. That's just 37°C away from being the lowest possible temperature in the entire Universe!**

Neptune's windy surface

Is it true?

Triton is Neptune's only moon.

NO. Neptune has seven other moons, but Triton and Nereid are the main ones. Triton is the biggest. It is 2,706 km across – about four-fifths the size of our Moon.

Where would you find pink snow?

When the gas nitrogen freezes, it looks like pink snow! There is frozen nitrogen at Neptune's north and south poles, and at the poles of its largest moon, Triton. So far from the Sun, Neptune and its moons are bitterly cold places.

Neptune seen from Triton

Pluto's icy surface is minus 220°C

Which is the coldest planet?

Pluto is the coldest planet of all, which is not surprising, because it is usually the furthest from the Sun. Inside, it is made up of ice and rock, and the planet has a thick layer of ice over the top.

Is it true?

Pluto was named after a cartoon dog.

NO. Pluto was the name of the Greek god of the underworld. Also, the first two letters of Pluto, 'P' and 'L' are the initials of Percival Lowell, who first predicted a planet beyond Neptune.

Who found Pluto's moon?

An American called Jim Christy discovered Pluto's moon in 1978. He called it Charon, which was his wife's name, and also the name of the man who ferried people to the underworld in Ancient Greek mythology.

Is Pluto always furthest from the Sun?

Pluto is so far away from the Sun that it takes 248 years just to orbit it once! But Pluto's orbit is a funny shape. For 20 years of its orbit, Pluto dips in closer to the Sun than Neptune. When this happens, Neptune is the furthest planet in the Solar System.

Amazing! Pluto is smaller than a country. Pluto is a dwarf planet. At 1,463 miles across, it is smaller than the United States or Russia!

Are there snowballs in space?

Yes – comets are balls of ice and rock. They go whizzing through the Solar System leaving behind a glowing tail of gas. As a comet gets closer to the Sun, it gets hotter and its tail becomes longer. Some comets even grow a second tail. In the past, the arrival of a comet was thought to be a magical event.

Amazing! **We can tell when comets will come back. Some comets follow a regular course, so we know exactly when we'll next see them. Halley's Comet will next fly past the Earth in 2061.**

Are there any other planets?

There are lots of minor planets, known as asteroids, in our Solar System. About 3,500 of these lumps of space rock are orbiting the Sun.

Asteroids orbiting the Sun

Is it true?

Asteroids weigh the same as the Earth.

NO. **Even if all of the asteroids in the Solar System were lumped together, the Earth would still weigh more than a thousand times as much.**

Comet with its glowing tail

What is a shooting star?

A shooting star, or meteor, happens when a tiny space rock, called a meteoroid, enters Earth's atmosphere and burns up. We see it as a streak of light across the sky. Meteor showers happen when our planet passes through a group of meteoroids.

Shooting stars

СССР
СССР

CHAPTER TWO

SPACE EXPLORATION

Who made the first rockets?

The Chinese made the first 'rockets' about 1,000 years ago, but they were more like fireworks than today's space rockets. They were flaming arrows that were fired from a basket using gunpowder.

Amazing! You don't need to be a rocket scientist to build rockets. Lots of people make mini rockets as a hobby. There is even a yearly contest, when people show off their latest creations!

Chinese 'rocket'

Is it true?
Thrust SSC is a rocket-powered car.

NO. Thrust SSC, the fastest car, has two jet engines. A jet engine could not power a space mission, because it needs air and there's no air in space.

When did the first liquid-fuel rocket fly?

In 1926, American Robert Goddard launched a 3.5 metre-long rocket. It flew about as high as a two-storey house, nowhere near outer space, and landed 56 metres away. The flight lasted just two-and-a-half seconds.

Who built a rocket for war?

Wernher von Braun invented the V2, a rocket missile used by the Germans in World War II. After the war, von Braun moved to the United States, to help with the new American space programme.

Why do we need rockets?

Rockets are important for space travel. They are the only machines powerful enough to launch things into space, such as satellites, probes and people. All the parts needed to build space stations have been carried up by rockets.

Ariane releasing a satellite

Amazing! **The European Ariane rocket could carry a fully grown elephant. Ariane's biggest payload (cargo) so far was a satellite which weighed 4.6 tonnes.**

How fast can a rocket go?

To escape from Earth's gravity, a rocket has to reach 40,000 kph – almost 20 times faster than supersonic Concorde. Once it is out in space, the rocket drops down to around 29,000 kph to stay in orbit.

Saturn 5 rocket

Rocket stages falling away

Is it true?

Saturn 5 rockets were as tall as a 30-storey building.

YES. At 111 metres high, the Saturn 5 was the tallest rocket ever made. Most of the rocket fell away once it had done its job.

Why do rockets fall to pieces?

Rockets are made in stages, or pieces. Usually, there are three stages, made up of the fuel and rocket engines. Each stage drops off when its job is done. It takes a huge amount of power to push a heavy rocket into space.

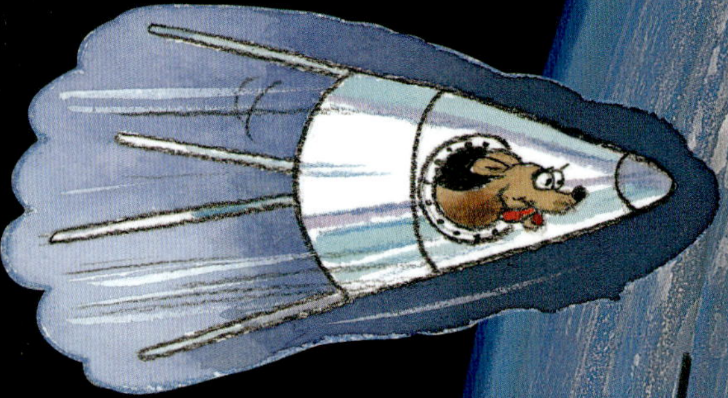

Amazing! The first living creature in space was a Russian dog, called Laika. She made a seven-day journey in the space capsule Sputnik 2 in November 1957.

Voskhod spacecraft

Yuri Gagarin and Vostok 1

Who was the first man in space?

A young Russian pilot called Yuri Gagarin was the first person in space. He orbited the Earth in a small capsule called Vostok 1 on 12 April 1961. His journey lasted less than two hours.

Who was the first woman in space?

The first woman in space was Russian, too. Valentina Tereshkova made a three-day space journey in Vostok 6 in 1963. The first American woman in space was Sally Ride, in 1983.

Valentina Tereshkova

Alexei Leonov making the first spacewalk

Who took the first spacewalk?

The cosmonaut (Russian astronaut) Alexei Leonov took a ten-minute spacewalk on 18 March 1965. To make sure he didn't float off, Leonov tied himself to his capsule.

Is it true?

A chimp could survive a space flight.

YES. Ham was the first to try out the Mercury capsule in 1961. Despite travelling at 8,045 kph, the chimpanzee survived the 16-minute flight.

Vostok capsule returning to Earth

Which astronauts went to sea?

American astronauts returning to Earth landed in the sea and were picked up by helicopter. Their capsules had huge parachutes to slow down their fall and rubber rings, so that they would float.

Apollo capsule splashing down

Amazing! **Capsules got extremely hot. When a capsule re-entered Earth's atmosphere, its surface heated it up to 3,000°C – twice the temperature needed to melt iron. But they didn't melt, because they were protected by a special heat shield.**

Who came down to Earth with a bang?

Russian capsules landed on hard ground. The cosmonauts bailed out and parachuted down the last few kilometres, but even so, many broke a few bones. They usually had to spend months in the hospital recovering from the landing!

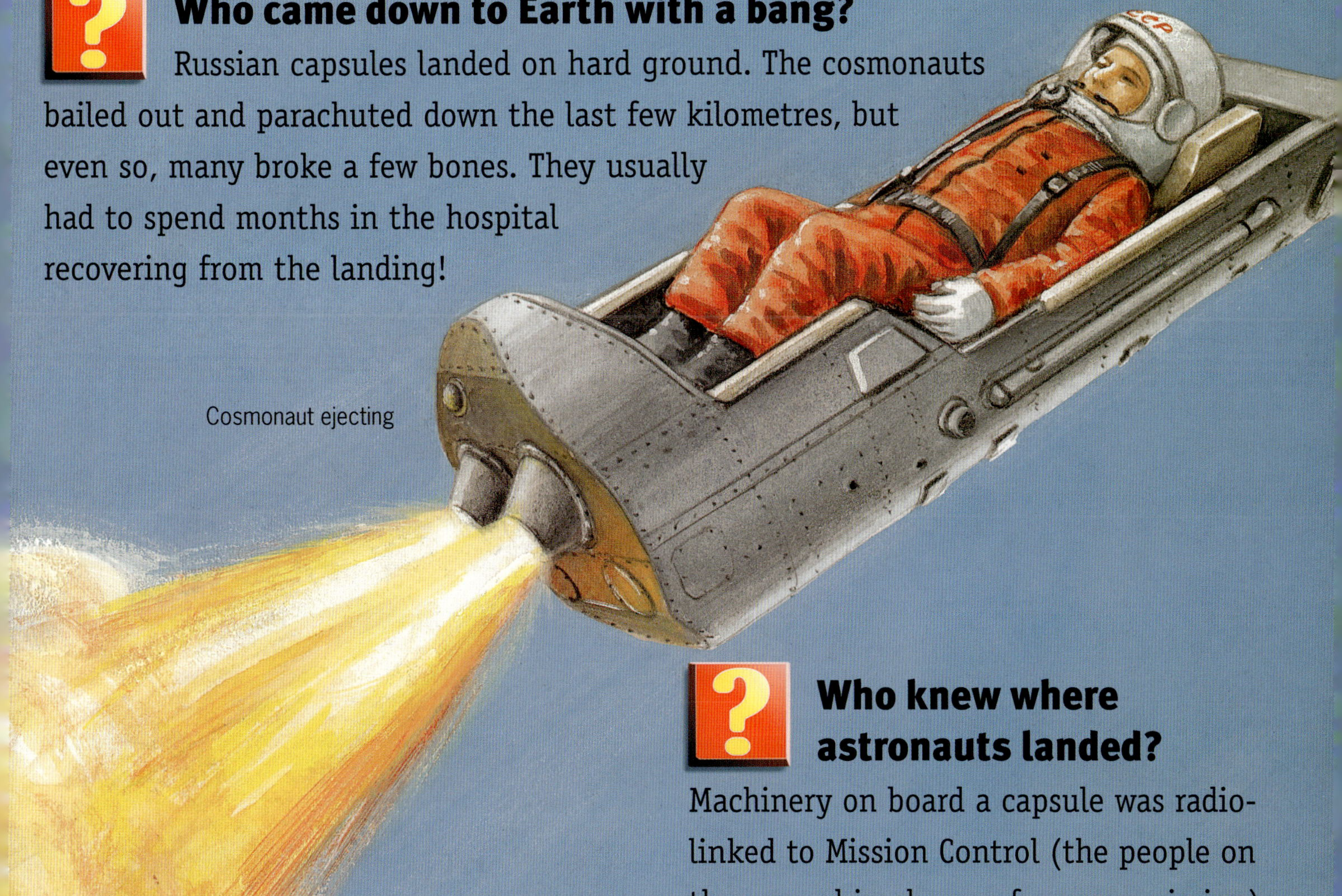

Cosmonaut ejecting

Who knew where astronauts landed?

Machinery on board a capsule was radio-linked to Mission Control (the people on the ground in charge of a space mission). This meant people knew exactly where to find the astronauts – usually!

Is it true?

Voskhod 2 got lost.

YES. Voskhod 2 was the capsule carrying Alexei Leonov, the first spacewalker. The auto-pilot machinery went wrong, and the capsule ended up 1,000 km off-course, in a snowy forest!

Mission Control

Neil Armstrong

Who first set foot on the Moon?

The very first person to step on to the Moon was the American Neil Armstrong, in 1969. He had flown there in Apollo 11 with Buzz Aldrin, who followed him on to the Moon's surface, and Michael Collins.

Apollo 13

Amazing! There should have been seven manned missions to the Moon. Two days into Apollo 13's journey to the Moon, its oxygen tanks exploded. It took a nail-biting four days to bring its crew safely back to Earth.

How many Moon missions were there?

There were six manned Apollo landings on the Moon, and about 80 unmanned ones too. Apollo 17 landed the last astronauts on the Moon in 1972.

Is it true?

There are footsteps on the Moon.

YES. There is no atmosphere on the Moon, which means there is no wind either. Tyre tracks and footprints in the dusty surface will be there for hundreds of years.

Who first drove on the Moon?

In 1971, Apollo 15 carried a Lunar Rover. David Scott and James Irwin drove the battery-powered buggy over the Moon's cratered surface, collecting samples of Moon rock.

Is it true?

There was only room for five astronauts aboard the shuttle.

NO. The space shuttle was designed to carry eight astronauts, but it can carry ten at a pinch!

The shuttle was launched using two solid rocket boosters and three main rocket engines

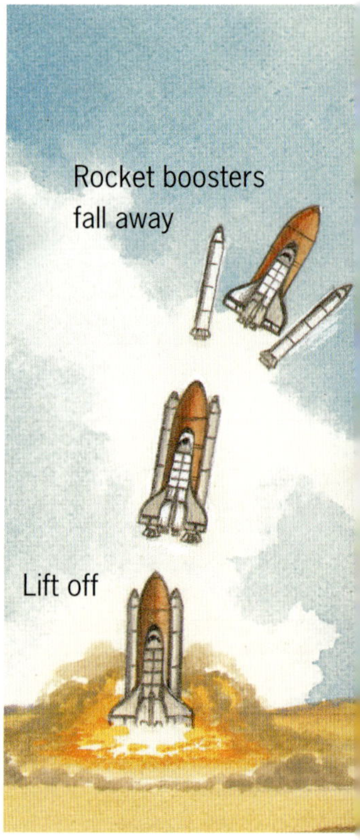

What was the first reusable spacecraft?

The space shuttle was the first spacecraft designed to be used more than once. Not every part was re-usable, because it needed new rocket boosters for each flight. The shuttles made over 100 missions into space. The first was Columbia, which blasted off in 1981. It orbited the Earth at about 27,840 kph – about ten times faster than a speeding bullet.

Challenger explosion

Are there any space shuttles in use today?

There are no shuttles in use today and some of them did not survive their missions. The shuttle challenger exploded shortly after lift off in 1986, and the shuttle Columbia disintegrated re-entering the Earth's atmosphere in 2003. Shuttles were used for launching and repairing satellites, and space research.

Amazing! **The Russian space shuttle, called Buran, only flew once, in 1988. Buran was carried into space by a rocket. Unlike the American shuttle, it was unmanned.**

How did the shuttle land?

At the end of its mission, the shuttle drops its speed to break orbit – on the opposite side of the world to the place it wants to land. Then it turns off its engines and glides like a bird, landing on a runway about an hour later.

Why do astronauts wear space suits?

Space suits act like a suit of armour. They stop an astronaut's blood boiling in space, and reflect the Sun's dangerous rays. They have a built-in backpack, containing an oxygen supply, battery and cooling system.

Amazing! **Astronauts are water-cooled! A system of tubes sewn into the space suit carries cool liquid around to keep the astronaut's temperature normal.**

Cosmonaut in space capsule

Is it true?
Cosmonauts took off in their underwear.

YES. **In the early days of Russian space travel, space suits were worn only for spacewalks. Some cosmonauts just wore their underwear at take-off time!**

Do astronauts wear space suits all the time?

No. They wear them for spacewalks and during take-off, landing or when they dock with another craft. The rest of the time, astronauts wear shorts and a tee shirt.

Backpack contains oxygen, batteries and water-cooling system

Shuttle astronaut putting on space suit

How do you go to the toilet in a space suit?

Astronauts often need to wee during take-off! Women wear an extra-absorbent nappy inside their suit. Some men prefer to do this too, but others wear a special sleeve that carries wee to a storage pouch inside the suit.

What's on the menu in space?

Astronauts either add water to waterless food, or they eat ready meals, such as stew or pasta. Canned fruit, puddings, biscuits, sweets and gum are all on the menu, too.

Space shuttle galley

Is it true?

Astronauts eat freeze-dried ice cream.

NO. The 'astronaut ice cream' sold in the shops isn't really eaten in space. But on the Mir space station, American astronauts took out an ice-cream feast to share with the Russian cosmonauts!

Eating in space

Why doesn't the food float away?

Everything floats about in space, so meals are eaten from trays stuck to astronauts' clothes. Drinks come in a cup with a lid and are sucked up through a straw.

Amazing! Some astronauts get space sickness! Floating makes many astronauts throw up, and if they're not careful the sick flies everywhere! Luckily, the sickness wears off after a day or two.

Skylab shower

How do astronauts wash?

The Skylab space station had a shower fitted with a vacuum cleaner to suck off the water, but there's no room for a shower on the shuttle. Astronauts use wet wipes, and clean their hair with rinseless shampoo.

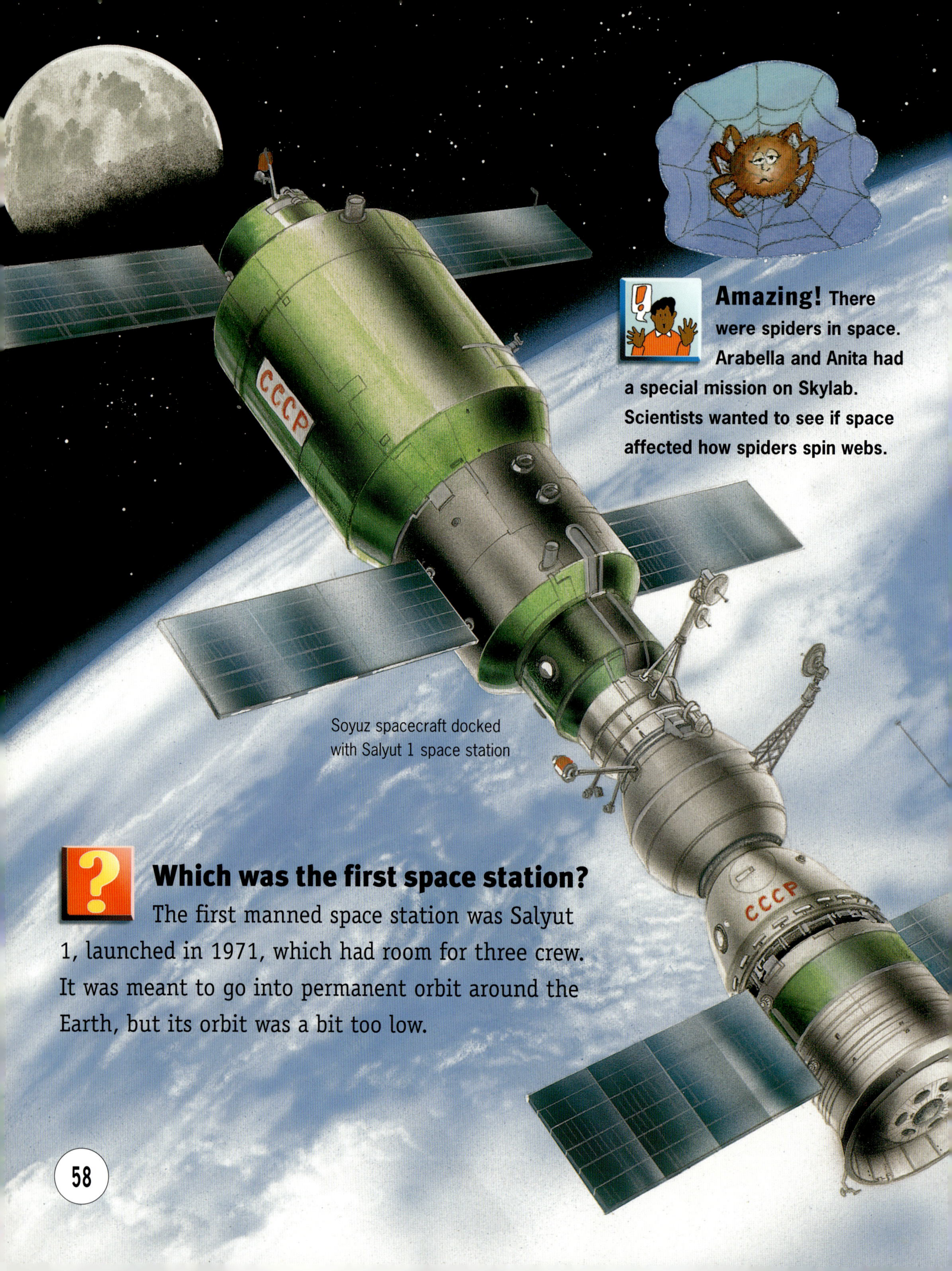

Soyuz spacecraft docked with Salyut 1 space station

Amazing! There were spiders in space. Arabella and Anita had a special mission on Skylab. Scientists wanted to see if space affected how spiders spin webs.

Which was the first space station?

The first manned space station was Salyut 1, launched in 1971, which had room for three crew. It was meant to go into permanent orbit around the Earth, but its orbit was a bit too low.

Exercise in space

What happens in a space station?

Astronauts live in space stations for weeks or even months. They do experiments and find out more about space. They also do lots of exercise, to stay fit and healthy.

Is it true?

Your bones get weaker in space.

YES. This isn't serious on short missions, but no one knows what would happen if you spent years in space.

Which is the biggest space station?

The International Space Station (ISS) is the biggest space station. Its parts were built by 16 countries.

International Space Station

Who needs a tool kit in space?

Astronauts need tools to build the ISS and repair satellites. In 1993, a space shuttle crew repaired the Hubble Space Telescope.

Working in space

MMU in action

What's an MMU?

MMU stands for Manned Manoeuvring Unit. It's like an armchair that carries an astronaut around in space, when he or she is outside the spacecraft. It uses 24 little gas jets to move backwards or forwards, up or down.

Is it true?

The space shuttle has an arm.

YES. It has a robot arm with a hand that can grip at the end. It can be controlled by astronauts inside or outside the shuttle. The robot arm is useful for picking up objects in space.

Amazing! Astronauts train underwater. Working underwater gives astronauts an idea of how it will feel to float in space. Water makes an astronaut's body move in the opposite direction when they try to pull or push something, just as it would in space.

Astronaut using headset radio

How do astronauts talk to each other?

Space is an airless vacuum that won't carry sound. Even if they were yelling, astronauts outside their craft wouldn't be able to hear each other, so they stay in touch by radio.

Has anyone ever been to Mars?

No, not yet, anyway! The distance from Earth to Mars varies from 56 million km to 400 million km. Even at its closest, Mars would be a six-month journey away.

Pathfinder landing

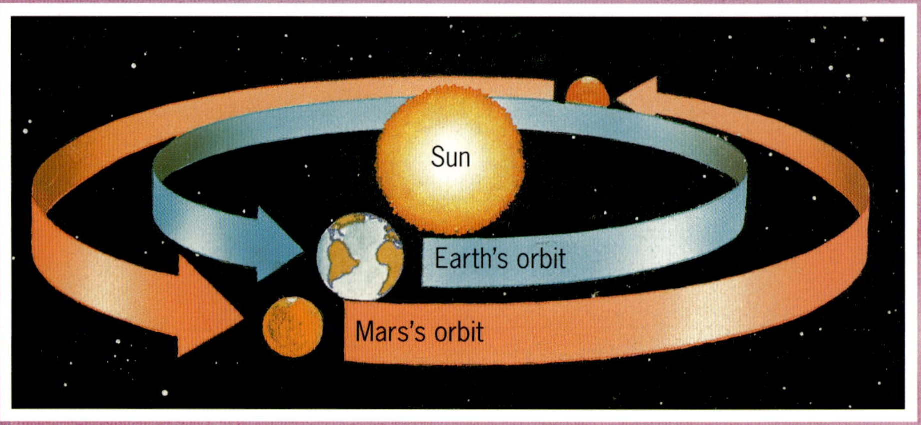

Is it true?

Vikings landed on Mars.

YES. In 1976, two space probes called Vikings 1 and 2 landed there. During their mission, they collected samples and took over 3,000 photos.

What used balloons to land on Mars?

The Mars Pathfinder probe entered the Martian atmosphere on 4 July 1997. It used a parachute and rockets to slow down and then a bundle of balloons inflated around it so that it could bounce safely down on to the surface.

Amazing! Pathfinder landed in a river! Although there is no liquid water on Mars now, the rocky plain where Pathfinder touched down showed signs that water had flowed there once.

Which robot explored Mars?

Pathfinder carried a robot car called Sojourner, which was radio-controlled from Earth. It had a camera and devices for studying the soil and rock.

Which was the first satellite in space?

Sputnik 1 was the first satellite to orbit the Earth. It was launched by the Russians in October 1957 and took 90 minutes to circle the planet.

Is it true?

A person could have fitted in Sputnik 1.

NO. The satellite was less than 60 cm across – smaller than most beach balls! Sputnik was just a radio transmitter really, but it was very important for space exploration.

Can you see any satellites from Earth?

Yes. You can see satellites moving across the sky when the Sun is shining on them but it is dark on Earth. The best times to spot satellites are the two hours after sunset and the two hours before sunrise.

Amazing! Satellites are powered by the Sun. Rocket power takes satellites up into orbit, but once they're there, they use special solar panels to collect energy from the Sun. This is turned into electricity to power the satellites' batteries.

Solar Maximum satellite

Why don't satellites fall down?

Earth's gravity tries to pull a satellite down, but the satellite's speed as it orbits the Earth tries to fling it into space. Usually, the two forces cancel each other out – but there have been mistakes!

Which probe snapped a comet?

The Giotto space probe visited Halley's Comet in 1986 and took brilliant photos of the comet's rocky core. Even though Giotto kept a safe distance of about 600 km, its special protective shields got covered in icy dust.

Amazing! **A probe carries a message for aliens. The Pioneer 10 probe was fitted with a plaque, just in case it's ever found by aliens. It shows a man and woman, and a map to show where Earth is in the Universe.**

Pioneer 10's plaque

Is it true?
A probe was made out of junk.

YES. **Magellan, sent to visit Venus in 1989, was made up of spare parts from other missions.**

Voyager 2 passing Jupiter

Which spacecraft flew farthest?

Voyager 2, launched in 1977, has flown past Jupiter, Saturn, Uranus and Neptune. Now it is beyond our Solar System, heading into interstellar space.

Cassini

Which probe is as big as a bus?

The bus-sized Cassini space probe has another probe, called Huygens, on board. Cassini has been studying the planet Saturn, and beams data back to Earth about Saturn's rings, moons, and the planet itself.

Moon Base of the future

Is it true?

We could never breathe on Mars.

NO. We couldn't breathe in the atmosphere there as it is, but we could build airtight cities and grow plants there that would make oxygen for us.

Might there be pirates in space?

If we ever set up space mining stations, spacecraft would zoom about the Solar System with very valuable cargos. Space pirates might try to board cargo-carrying craft to rob them!

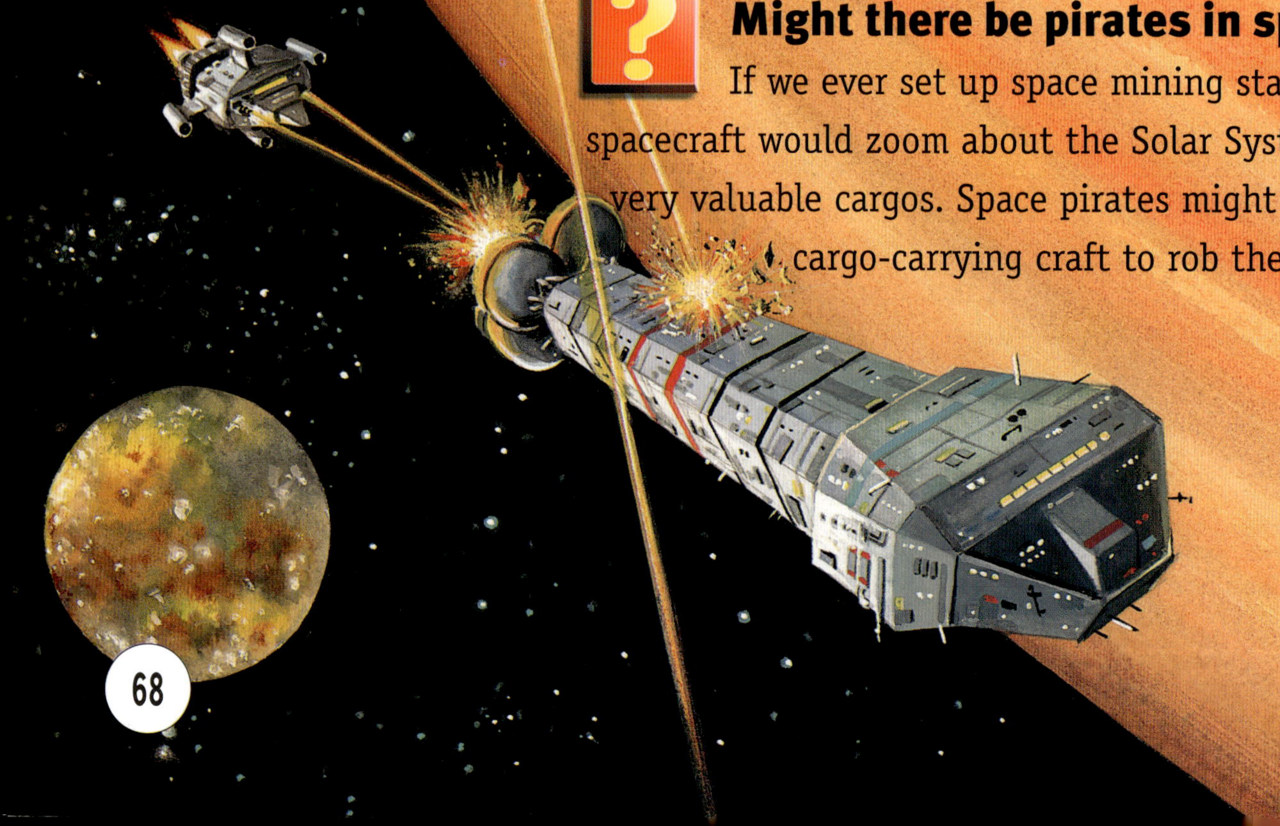

Will we ever live on the Moon?

There might be a Moon Base, one day. The Moon is only three days away and its low gravity makes it easy to land spacecraft there. It would be a good place for telescopes, because there is no atmosphere to distort the pictures.

Amazing! People are planning a space hotel. Holidays in space are not far off. There are plans for a doughnut-shaped space hotel, using old shuttle fuel tanks as rooms!

Will we ever live on other planets?

It will take a lot more probe missions before we could consider building bases on other planets. But if travel to other stars ever became possible, the outer planets could act as useful 'petrol stations'.

Space tanker near Saturn

CHAPTER THREE

BEYOND OUR SOLAR SYSTEM

What is the Universe?

Every person, planet, star and galaxy is part of the Universe – and even every empty space! The Universe is the biggest thing we have a word for.

Amazing! **The Universe is too big to measure in kilometres. Even if you could travel at the speed of light, it would take at least 15 billion years to cross it – as far as we know!**

What's outside the Universe?

It's impossible to say. Scientists are still trying to guess, by using clues left behind from the birth of our Universe. They are pretty sure there would be no time, distance or things there.

Where are we in the Universe?

People once thought Earth was at the centre of the Universe. Now we know Earth is one of many planets moving through space. It's hard to tell where we are because we can't see the Universe's edges.

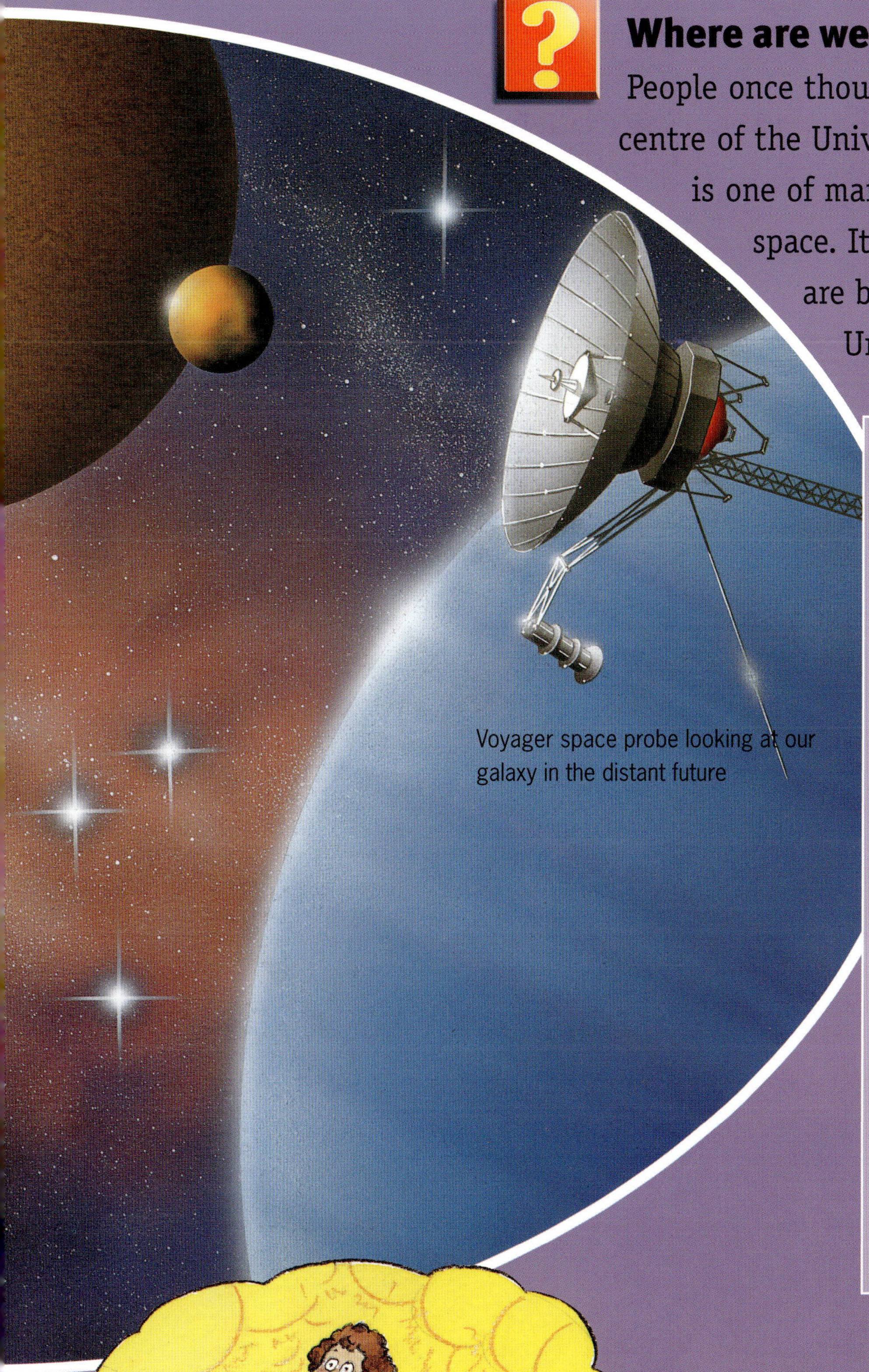

Voyager space probe looking at our galaxy in the distant future

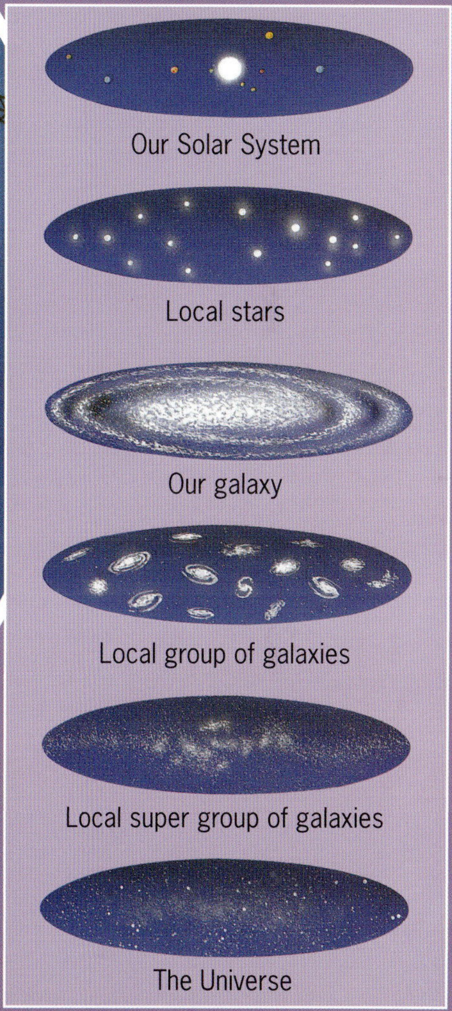

Is it true?

There are more stars than people.

YES. As a rough guess, scientists think that there are about 1.8 million million stars for every human being alive in the world today.

The Universe expands from the Big Bang

When did the Universe begin?

Scientists have argued about this for centuries. At the moment, most people agree that the Universe began between 12 and 15 billion years ago. It all started with a mind-boggling explosion called the Big Bang.

Amazing! **The Big Bang was super-hot! Scientists don't even bother writing out all the zeros in its temperature. They write 10^{27}°C, meaning 10 with 27 zeros after it!**

What was the Big Bang?

It was a huge explosion, that created all the mass and energy in our Universe in less than a second! The effects of the blast are so strong that the Universe is still expanding.

Is it true?

You could see the Big Bang through a telescope.

NEARLY. Our telescopes aren't powerful enough yet – but we can already see light from the other side of the Universe that began its journey just after the Big Bang!

What if the Big Bang happened again?

It couldn't happen again in our Universe, but some people think it may be happening millions of times, making millions of different universes. Only a few would last as long as ours – most would pop like soap bubbles.

There might be millions of universes

Will the Universe ever end?

Some cosmologists (people who study the Universe) believe that the Universe will eventually stop expanding outwards. They think it will shrink back to nothing in an event called the Big Crunch!

Is it true?
The Universe might just fizzle out.

YES. If the Universe keeps spreading out forever, it will get quite boring. After the stars have burnt out, there'll just be lumps of rock and dust floating around doing nothing!

The Universe shrinks back to the Big Crunch

Why would it crunch?

The Universe is still blowing up, but there are lots of heavy things in it. Just like a toy balloon, which has run out of puff, gravity might pull the Universe back to where, and how, it started.

Amazing! **The Universe might go on forever! Some cosmologists think that the Universe will never stop expanding. They don't think gravity will ever be able to stop it, so it will just get bigger and bigger.**

Will I see the Big Crunch?

Not unless you live forever! Even if the Universe does stop expanding, it will take about another 15 billion years to collapse in on itself in a Big Crunch.

What are star nurseries?

New stars are born in star nurseries – huge clouds of gas and dust known as nebulae (or nebula if you're just talking about one). Nebulae are some of the most beautiful sights that powerful telescopes have ever revealed.

Stars are born in gaseous clouds called nebulae

Amazing! A star can be born in a horse's head! The Horsehead Nebula is a glowing cloud of gas in another galaxy. It has a lump shaped like a horse's head, where stars are being born.

How are stars born?

The gases in a nebula gradually gather together into spinning balls. They spin more and more quickly, until they get amazingly hot and a big blast, called a nuclear reaction, begins. When this happens, a baby star begins to glow.

What are stars made of?

Stars are mostly made of two gases, hydrogen and helium. Helium is the gas used to fill party balloons. There are lots of layers inside a star, with gases moving around in each one.

Is it true?
You are made of stardust.

YES. Everything in space, including you, is made out of elements, such as carbon and silicon. All of these were cooked up in stars, which formed from the first matter in the Universe.

Which stars live together?

Our star, the Sun, is all alone, but some stars, called binary stars, are in pairs. They seem to spin around each other. Very close pairs do one turn of this 'dance' in just hours!

Binary stars viewed from a planet in deepest space

Our Sun is a medium-sized star

How long do stars shine for?

It depends. Very hot, bright stars burn up all their energy in a few million years. A star like our Sun, which is only medium-hot, can shine for billions of years.

What is a white giant?

White giants are really huge, hot stars that appear to be white. They can be 20 times bigger than our Sun. Rigel is a white giant shining about 60,000 times more brightly than our Sun.

Our Sun compared to a white giant

Amazing! Small stars are called dwarfs! Astronomers know that stars come in lots of different sizes. To make it easier to describe the sizes, they call big stars giants and little ones dwarfs.

Is it true?
Most stars are yellow.

NO. Stars hotter than our Sun often shine a bright pale blue, while other stars can sometimes appear red or white. Only a few are yellow.

Which stars go out with a bang?

Really massive stars, at least eight times bigger than our Sun, die in an explosion called a supernova. For a few days supernovas shine so strongly that, here on Earth, we can see them during the day.

Amazing! Supernovas are a very rare sight. Only a few supernovas have been seen in our galaxy in the last 1,000 years. One visible to the naked eye was seen in 1987, in a nearby galaxy called the Large Magellanic Cloud.

What is a white dwarf?

A white dwarf is a dying star. Its gas has burnt off, and a planet-sized, white-hot and incredibly dense core is all that is left. Over billions of years, this fades and dies. Sirius B, or the 'Pup', is a white dwarf.

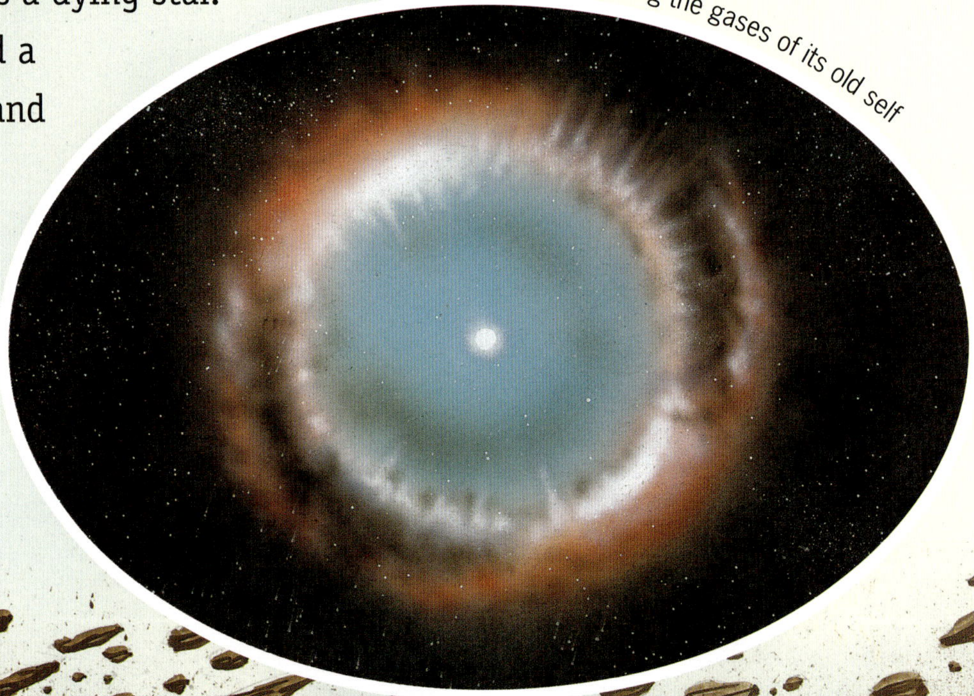

A white dwarf shedding the gases of its old self

What is a red giant?

A red giant is an old star that has swollen up. Depending how big it gets, it might blow up or fade out. Astronomers think that our Sun will grow into a red giant in about five billion years' time. Betelgeuse is a red giant, and is 500 times bigger than our Sun.

Our Sun compared to an enormous red giant

A red giant swallows up a planet

Is it true?

Dead stars are called black dwarfs.

YES. Once a white dwarf has cooled and stopped shining, it becomes a dead, black dwarf.

What is the LGM?

LGM stands for 'Little Green Man'. LGM1 is a light deep in space that flashes 30 times a second. It is a pulsar – a tiny, dense neutron star (the remains of a supernova) that flashes out light and radio signals as it spins.

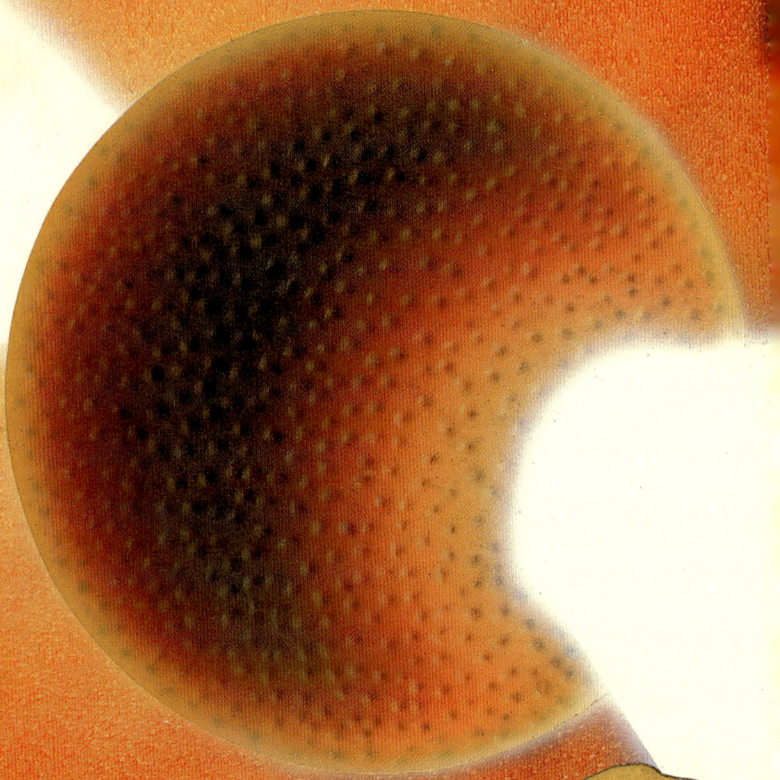

A pulsar flashing out light and radio signals, near a red giant

Is it true?

Scientists thought pulsar signals were messages from aliens.

YES. The astronomers in Cambridge, England, who discovered LGM1 wondered at first if they'd come across an alien distress beacon or some other kind of coded message!

AMAZING!

Neutron stars are super-heavy! They can be just 20 km across, but weigh 50 times more than planet Earth!

Radio telescopes

How many pulsars are there?

No one is sure, but hundreds have been found since the 1960s, when scientists first spotted the Little Green Man. Special telescopes called radio telescopes are used to 'listen' for more pulsars.

Do all pulsars spin at the same speed?

No – even the slowest spin about once every four seconds, but the fastest whizz round many hundreds of times in a single second! Their incredible speeds are thought to be caused by magnetic forces left by a supernova.

What is a black hole?

A black hole is a place in space that forms when a really huge star collapses. Everything around a black hole is sucked into it, like water down a plug hole. The force of gravity in a black hole is so strong that nothing can escape from it – not even light.

Amazing!

No one has ever seen a black hole. Because beams of light cannot escape black holes, astronomers cannot see them – even with the most powerful telescopes.

What is dark matter?

Dark matter is what scientists call all the stuff in the Universe that they know is there but can't find! They think it might be made of ghostly little particles called neutrinos.

Neutrinos

Is it true?

Black holes turn you into spaghetti.

YES. Scientists think that, in the last moments before you disappeared forever into a black hole, the force of gravity would stretch you until it pulled you apart. They call this being 'spaghettified'!

Dark matter

How do we know that dark matter is there?

Scientists can guess how much matter is in the Universe by measuring how galaxies move. This shows them that stars and planets only make up a small part of the Universe. The rest is invisible!

What is a galaxy?

A galaxy is a group of stars, dust and gases that are held together by gravity. Our galaxy is the Milky Way and contains about 100 billion stars, one of which is our Sun.

Is it true?

All galaxies have names.

NO. Each one that we detect is given numbers and letters, but only some, such as our Milky Way, are given a name as well. Galaxy comes from the Ancient Greek word for 'milk'.

On a clear night you can see the Milky Way

How many galaxies are there?

No one knows for sure. There might be hundreds of billions of galaxies – and new ones are forming right now at the edges of the Universe.

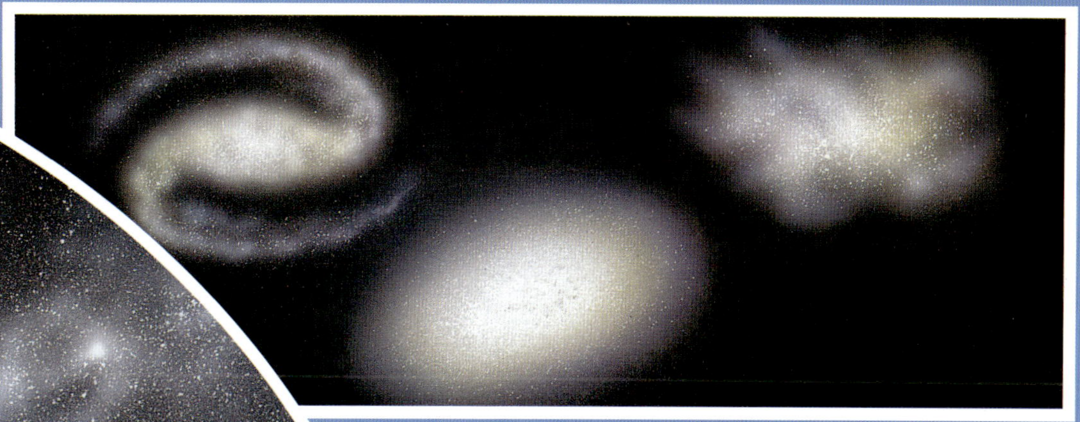

Spiral, oval and irregular galaxies

Are there different kinds of galaxies?

Yes – each galaxy is unlike any other. Some are bright and some are dim. There are three basic galaxy shapes, though – spiral, elliptical (oval) and irregular. Of course, irregular just means no particular shape!

Amazing!

There's a galaxy named after a wide-brimmed Mexican hat. 'Sombrero' is the nickname of galaxy M104. Can you guess the galaxy's shape?

Galaxies can form in many weird and wonderful shapes

What shape is our galaxy?

Our galaxy, the Milky Way, is a spiral galaxy. Viewed from above, it looks like a giant Danish pastry with swirls of white icing. From the side, it looks more like two fried eggs stuck back-to-back!

Amazing! **Our galaxy has a twin. Andromeda is the biggest galaxy near the Milky Way. It's the same age and a similar shape, but has many more stars.**

What's at the middle of the Milky Way?

The centre (the two 'egg yolks') is called the nuclear bulge. There's probably a monster black hole there, more than a million times bigger than our Sun. Scientists call the black hole Sagittarius A*.

A side view of the Milky Way seen from deep space

How big is the Milky Way?

The Milky Way is almost too big to imagine. It would take the world's fastest jet, the Blackbird, about 30 billion years to cross the galaxy.

Blackbird

Is it true?

We're near the centre of the Milky Way.

NO. Our Solar System is closer to the edge, on one of the spiralling arms. Our Sun takes 225 million years to go around the centre once!

Do galaxies stick together?

Some galaxies are all alone in space, but others huddle together in clusters. Together with 30 other galaxies, our Milky Way and its twin, Andromeda, are part of the Local Group cluster.

Cluster of galaxies

Are some galaxies cannibals?

Some scientists think that Andromeda gobbled up other galaxies. It has a double centre, which might be the remains of another galaxy. One day, Andromeda may eat up the Milky Way. It gets 300 km closer to us every second!

The background shows two galaxies colliding

Amazing!
The Local Supercluster contains several thousand galaxies, and is more than 100 million light years across. A light year is about 9,461 billion km.

What is a supercluster?

It's a cluster of clouds of clusters! The Local Group that contains our Milky Way is part of a cloud called the Canes Venatici cloud. Together with about six other clouds of galaxies, it is part of the Local Supercluster.

Supercluster of galaxies

Is it true?

We're part of the biggest galaxy cloud in the Local Supercluster.

NO. **The biggest is the Virgo I cloud, which contains a fifth of all the galaxies in the supercluster. It's pulling the other clouds in the cluster towards it.**

The Moon's gravity pulls a meteorite crashing into its surface

What is gravity?

Gravity is one of the basic forces in the Universe, like electromagnetism. It makes things with mass pull towards each other. More massive objects, such as the Earth, pull smaller objects, such as you, towards them until they stick together.

Is it true?

An apple taught us about gravity.

MAYBE. According to legend, super-scientist Isaac Newton first realized how gravity works nearly 350 years ago, after gravity pulled an apple from a tree he was sitting under, and it landed on his head!

Is the Universe expanding evenly?

No – the force of gravity stops everything from flying outwards. Lumpy bits of space become even lumpier, moving at different speeds. Gravity locks together little pockets of space and matter, such as galaxies.

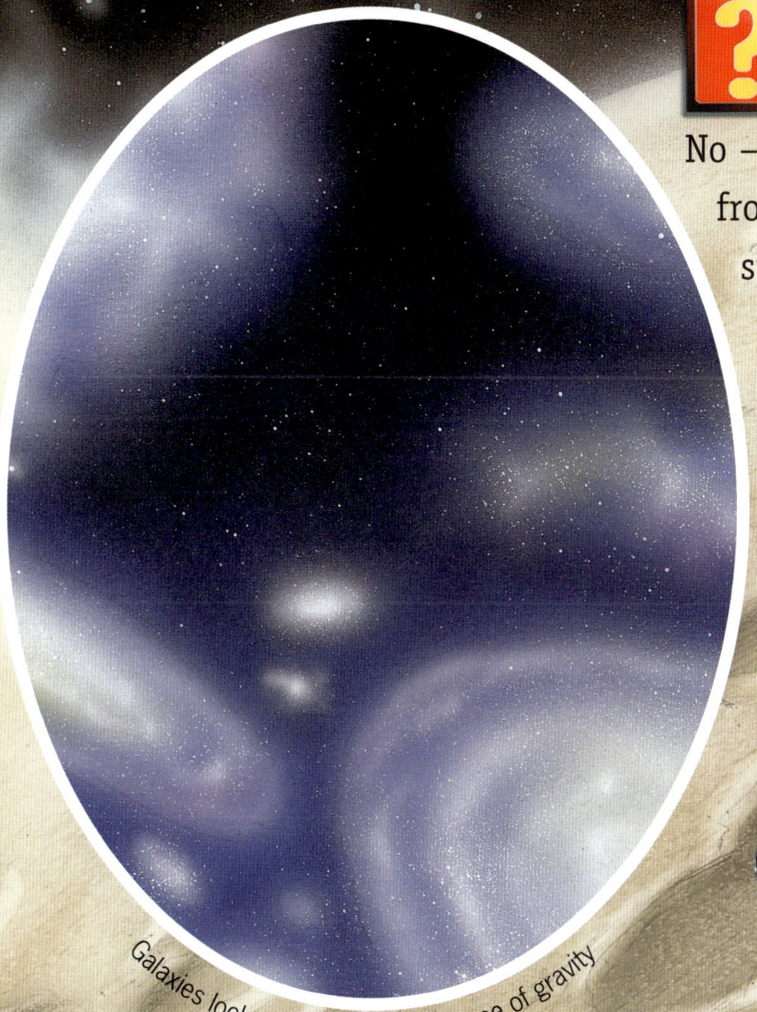

Galaxies locked together by the force of gravity

Amazing!

There are walls in space! Galaxies aren't evenly spaced through the Universe. They are arranged more like walls around emptier regions of space. One wall has already been measured – it's about a billion light years across!

What is the Great Attractor?

It's a strange little knot in space that has the pulling power of 50 million billion Suns, but is not a black hole.

Is time the same everywhere?

No, time slows down when you're travelling very quickly. Brainy boffin Albert Einstein predicted this odd effect in 1905 but we only proved it a few years ago by sending a super-precise atomic clock into orbit around the Earth.

Albert Einstein

Is it true?

Einstein was the world's best mathematician.

NO. Although he was very clever, Albert Einstein often asked his wife to check over the trickier sums for him.

A black hole

Could time stand still?

Only if you travelled as fast as the speed of light – which most scientists agree is impossible! Some scientists think that time must stand still inside a black hole, but who'd want to find out?

Amazing! There might be 'tunnels' through space and time, which connect distant parts of the Universe. Scientists call these shortcuts wormholes. If light or even an object entered a wormhole, perhaps it would pass through incredibly quickly. It would be possible to travel billions of kilometres in an instant!

Time travel to a different universe

Is time travel possible?

Not as far as we know. If you could invent a machine which seemed to take you back or forwards in time, it would probably be taking you to different universes.

Is there anybody out there?

We don't know. Life might be such a fluke that it only exists on Earth. But if scientists can find just one other place where there is life, we'll know life's no accident – and that there could be millions of aliens!

How will we find out?

People around the world have joined the Search for Extra-Terrestrial Intelligence (SETI). They spend their spare time on computers, studying waves from space, hoping to find alien messages.

Radio astronomy centre

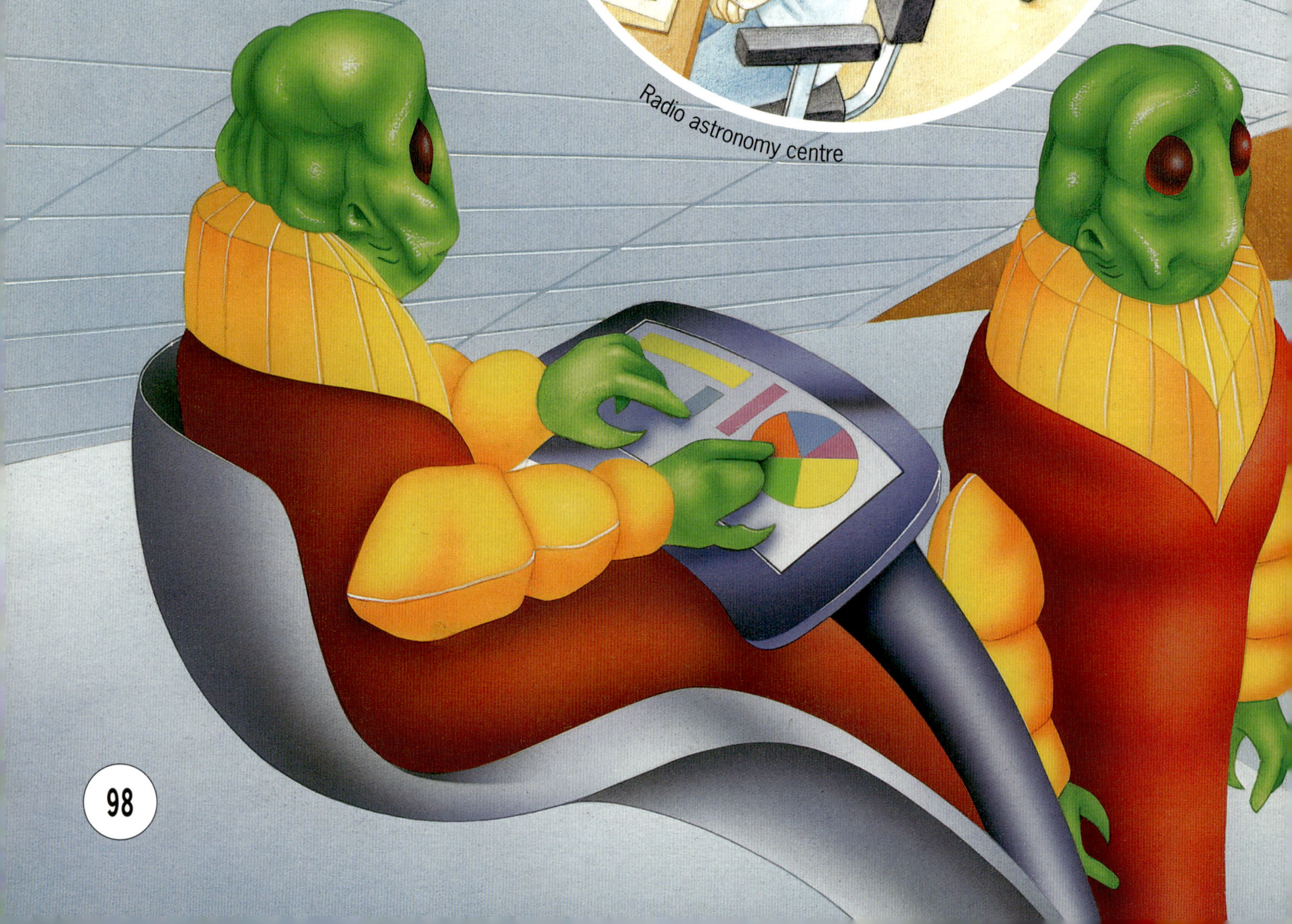

Do aliens know about us?

It's unlikely. Humans have only been making radio waves for about a century, so aliens would have to live very nearby to tune in.

Amazing! Some people think that the Universe is a living thing – and that the planets, stars and galaxies are just parts of its 'body'!

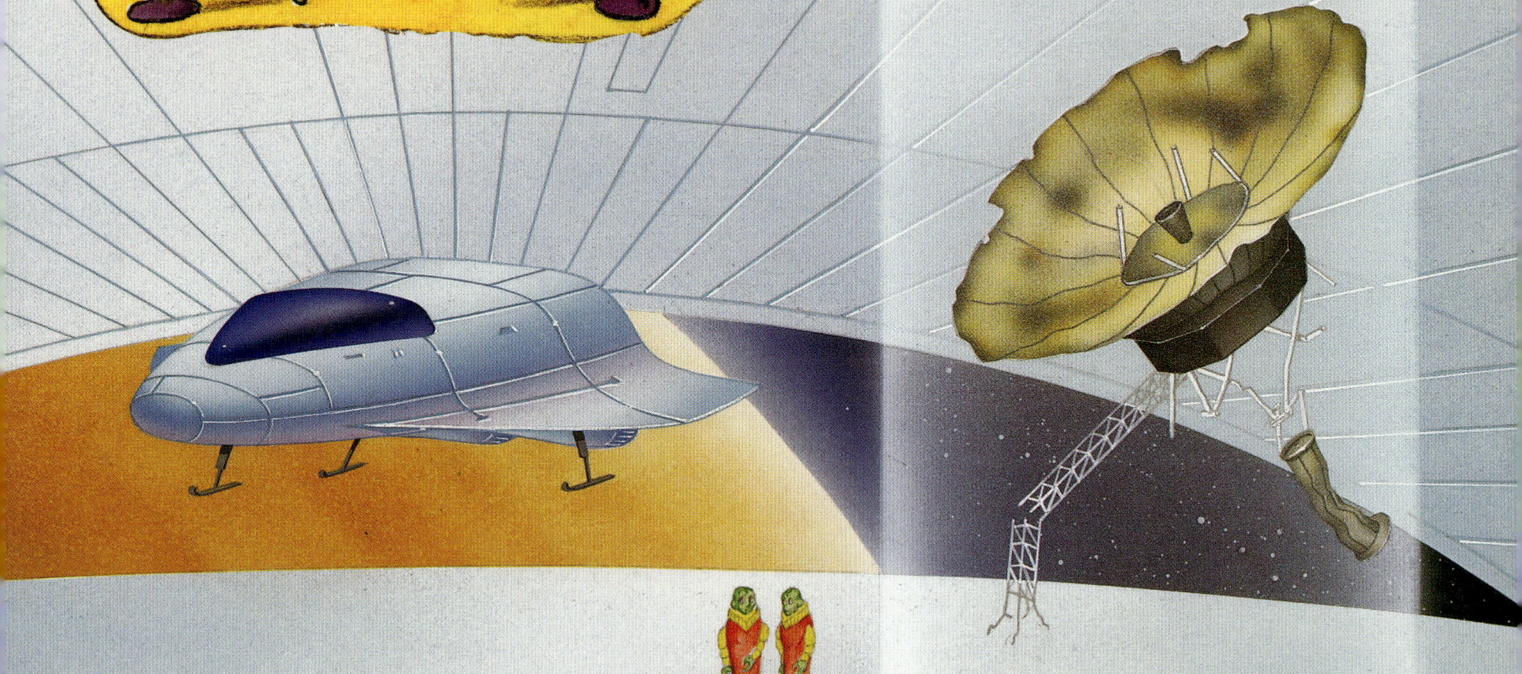

Aliens with the Pioneer space probe

Is it true?

Aliens have visited the Earth.

PROBABLY NOT. There's no proof that aliens have visited us. Even if they could travel at the speed of light, they would take at least four years to reach us from the nearest stars.

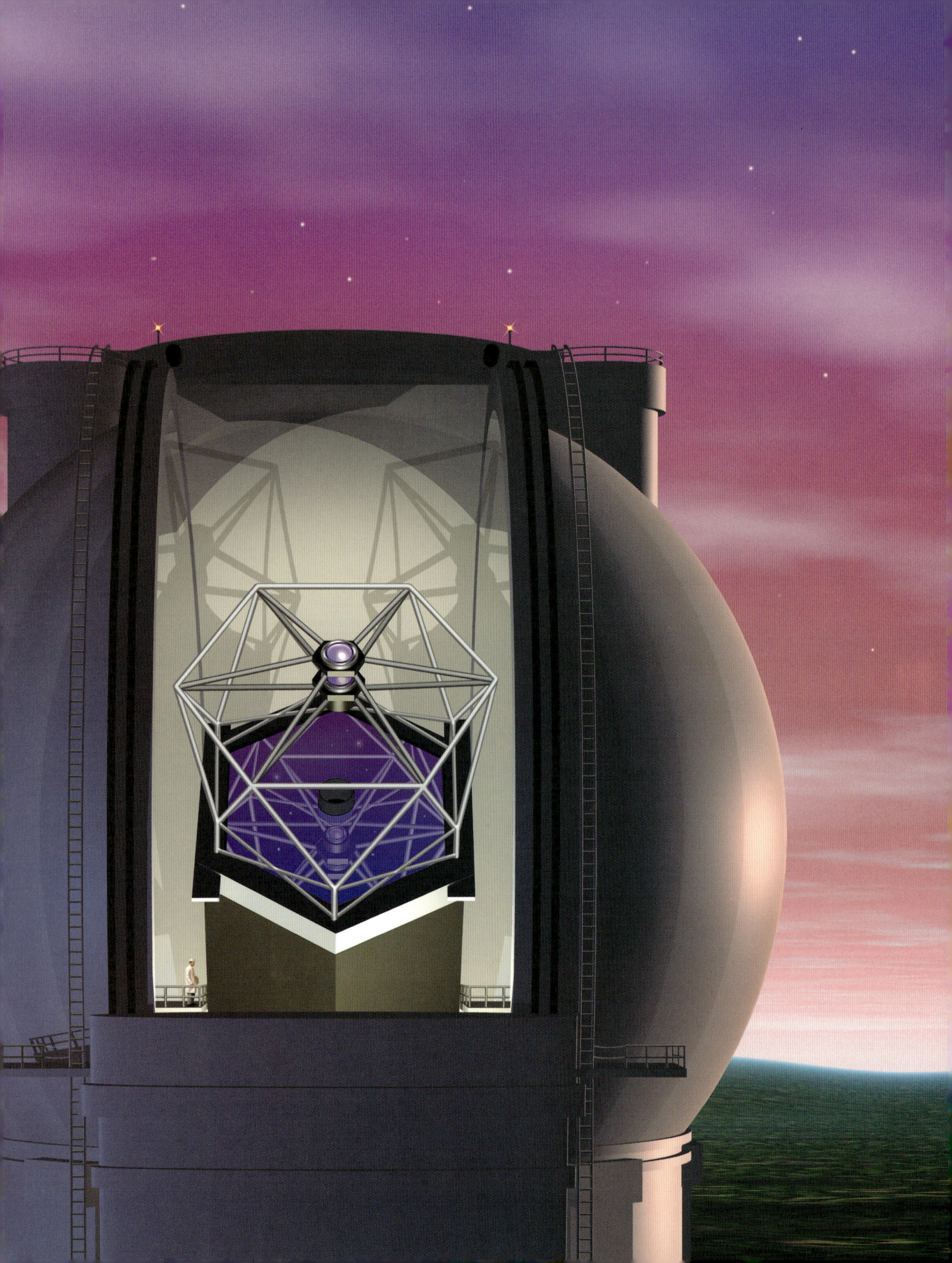

CHAPTER FOUR

LOOKING AT THE NIGHT SKY

Who gazes at the stars?

We all enjoy looking up at the starry night sky, especially on a clear moonless night, away from bright city lights. Some people even star-gaze as a job. They are scientists called astronomers. Astronomy is the science of studying space and all the objects in it.

Astronomer and telescope

Amazing! You can see about 2,500 stars in the night sky! When the sky is clear, you can see that many different stars even without a telescope!

Can anyone be an astronomer?

Anyone can learn about stars as a hobby, but it takes years of study to do it as a job. You'll need books of star charts and maps, so you can recognize what you see. Binoculars or a telescope will let you see further.

Studying a star chart

Is it true?

You can see the Moon's craters through binoculars.

YES. Binoculars allow you to see the Moon's surface so clearly that you can make out individual craters – from 400,000 km away!

Can you only see the Moon and stars at night?

The Moon and stars are easiest to spot, but even without a telescope you will see meteors (shooting stars) and the brighter planets, such as Venus, Jupiter or Mars. Venus shines white and is nicknamed the 'evening star'. Jupiter looks greeny-blue and Mars glows red.

Meteor shower

Who built a tomb for the Sun god?

The Ancient Egyptians thought their kings were the Sun god, Ra, who had come down to Earth. They buried kings in huge tombs called pyramids, maybe because the pyramid shape pointed at the sky.

Is it true?

Stonehenge was a primitive computer.

NO. But in the 1960s an American scientist called Gerald Hawkins said it was. He thought Stonehenge was built to work out when eclipses would happen.

Who built a stone circle for the Sun?

No one knows exactly why Stonehenge, a huge stone circle in southwest England, was built by Druids over 4,000 years ago. Its doorway would have framed the sunrise on the longest day of each year.

Who thought the sky was a goddess?

The Egyptians thought the night sky was the arched body of a goddess, called Nut. Today we know Nut's body matches the view of the Milky Way from Ancient Egypt.

The Milky Way seen above the pyramids

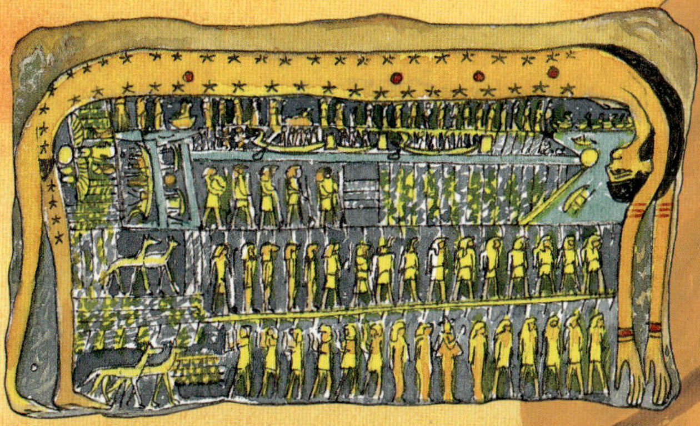
Ancient Egyptian wall painting showing the goddess Nut

Amazing!

The pyramids have secret Sun passages! Tunnels were built so the buried king could see the sunset on a particular day each spring.

Ancient Druid ceremony at Stonehenge

Who first wrote about the stars?

The Babylonians were the first to write down their findings from studying the stars – around 5,000 years ago! They noticed that stars seem to form patterns, which we call constellations. The Babylonian empire was roughly where Iraq is today.

Babylonian astromomers

Is it true?

The Babylonians were maths wizards.

YES. At first their findings about the night sky were based on looking and guessing. By around 500 BC, the Babylonians used sums to predict exactly when events such as eclipses would happen.

How do we know about the first astronomers?

The Babylonians didn't write on paper like we do. They wrote on clay tablets, so fragments have survived. Scientists called archaeologists dig in the ground for clues about ancient peoples such as the Babylonians.

Babylonian writing on a clay tablet

Amazing! **The Babylonians didn't see the same night sky as us. There were no twinkling satellites, and the stars were in different places because our Solar System has moved since then.**

Clay tablet

What was a Babylonian year like?

The Babylonians worked out a 12-month year. Each month began with the first sight of the crescent Moon. The months were called Nisannu, Ayaru, Simanu, Du'uzu, Abu, Ululu, Tashritu, Arahsamnu, Kislimu, Tebetu, Shabatu and Addaru.

Amazing! An eclipse changed the course of history. Soldiers from Athens in Ancient Greece lost a battle after being spooked by an eclipse of the Moon. Their rivals, the Spartans, were the winners.

? Who thought the Sun was as wide as a ruler?

The Greek thinker Heraclitus thought the Sun was just 30 cm across and that a new one was made each morning. So even though the Ancient Greeks were clever, they didn't get everything right!

Who named groups of stars?

In AD 150, the Greek astronomer Ptolemy wrote a book about the stars, describing 48 different constellations (star groups). He named the groups after characters from Greek myths, such as Perseus, the hero who rescued the princess Andromeda. We still use Ptolemy's names today.

Is it true?

People once thought the Earth was flat.

YES. Even up to the 1500s most people believed this. They thought that if you sailed too far, you could fall off the edge!

Aristotle

Who worked out the Earth is round?

The Ancient Greek thinker Aristotle realized that the Earth must be round in the 330s BC. He worked this out when he was watching a lunar eclipse, because he saw that the Earth made a circular shadow on the surface of the Moon.

Why do stars make patterns?

Constellations are the patterns that bright stars seem to make in the night sky, such as a cross, a letter 'W' or the shape of a person. The stars look close together – but that's just how we see them from Earth. Really they are scattered through space and nowhere near each other.

Amazing! **The night sky is divided into 88 different star patterns. Nearly 50 were first described 2,000 years ago!**

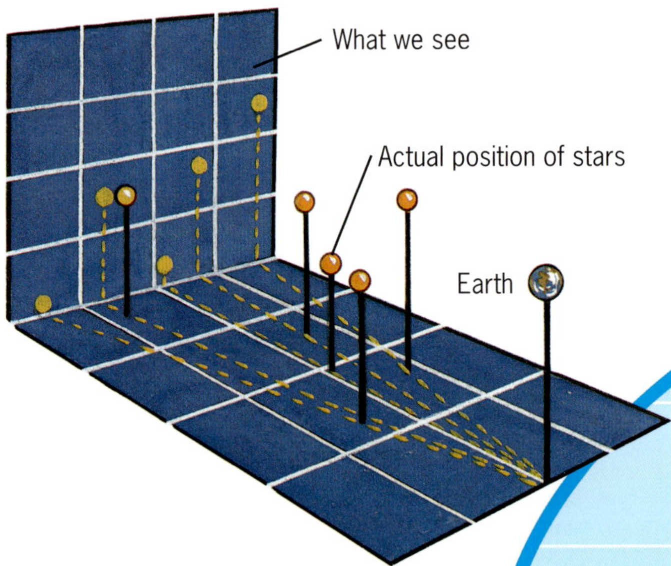

What is the zodiac?

For astronomers, the zodiac includes the 12 constellations that the Sun passes through during a year. We can't see the Sun doing this, though. The Sun's light is so bright that we cannot see the constellations during the day.

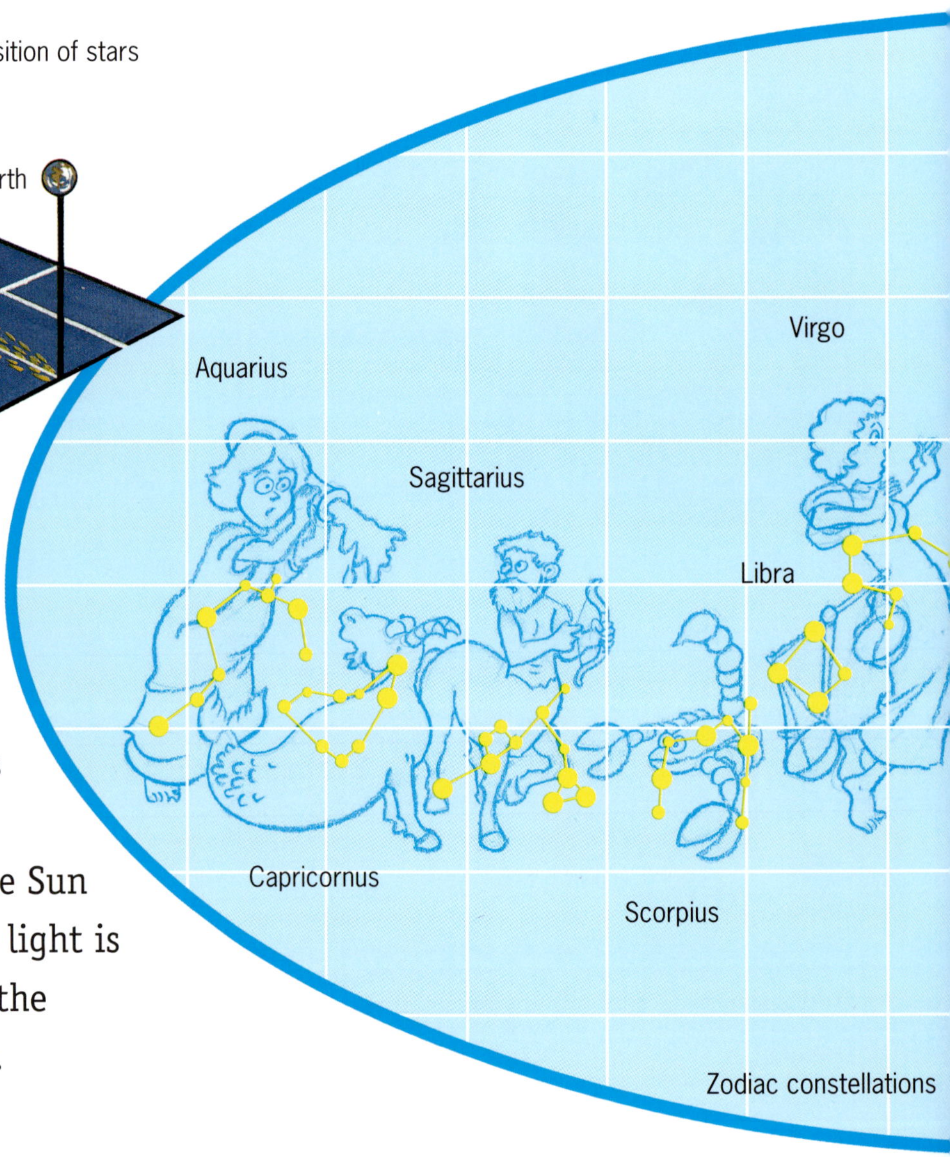

Which stars make a hunter?

Orion is a constellation named after the legendary Greek hunter. Lots of stars make up the shape. Rigel is the brightest and makes one of the hunter's legs. The next-brightest is Betelgeuse, which shines a reddish colour.

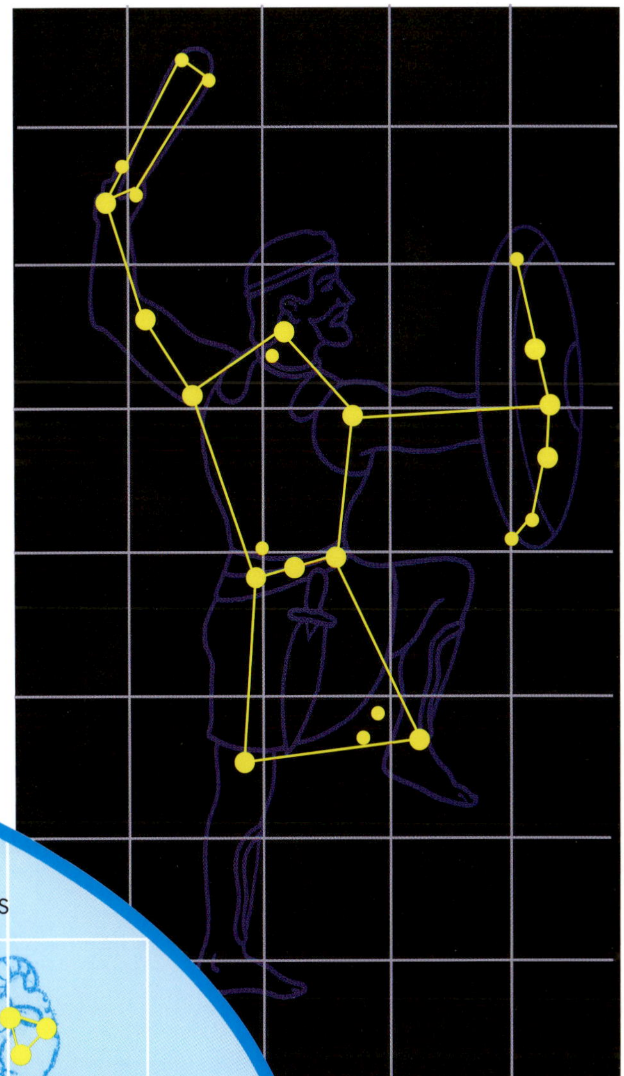

Orion

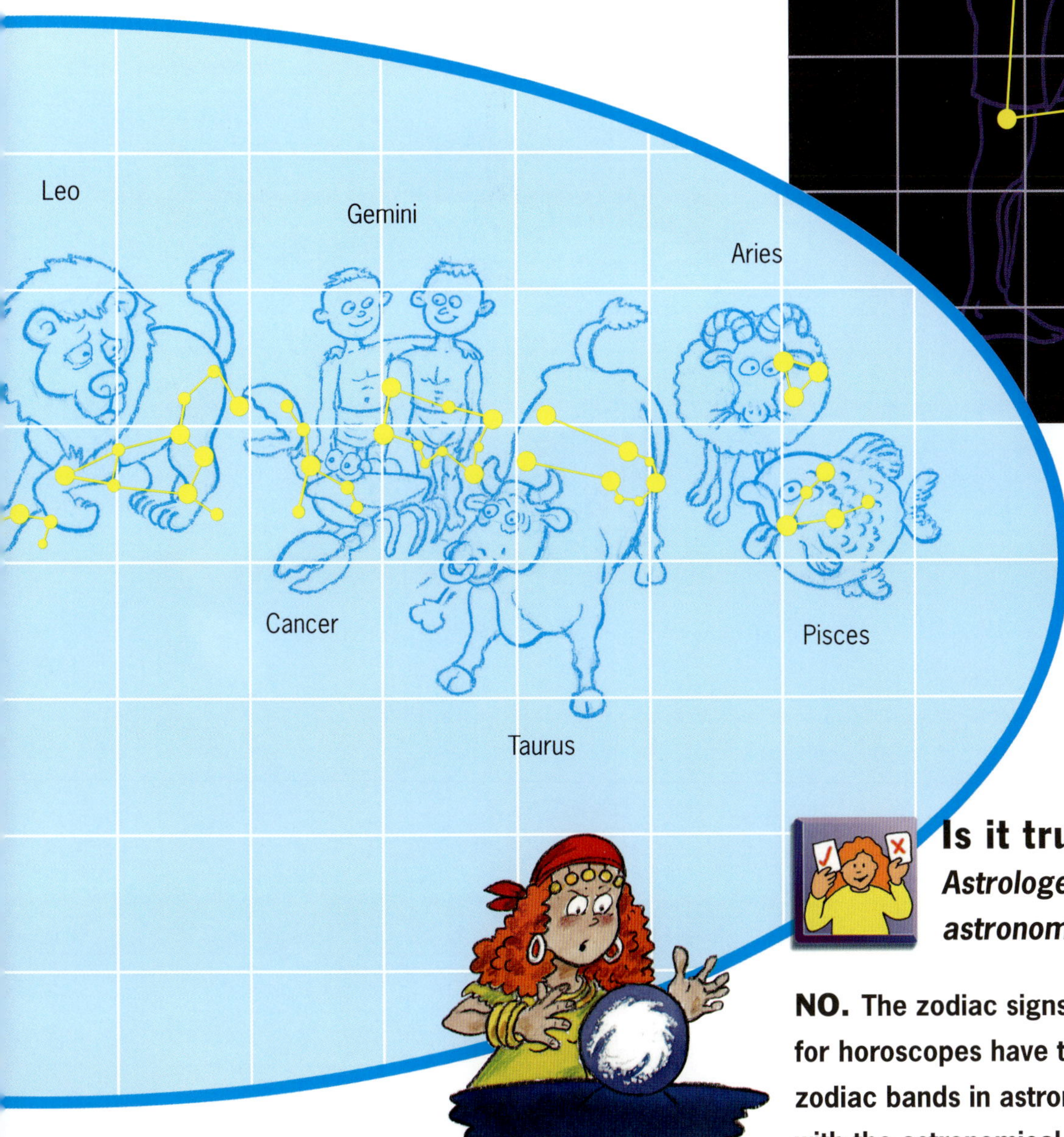

Is it true?

Astrologers are specialist astronomers.

NO. The zodiac signs that astrologers use for horoscopes have the same names as the zodiac bands in astronomy. They don't match with the astronomical constellations, though.

How did sailors know where they were going?

Out at sea, there are no landmarks. In the Middle Ages, sailors had special instruments that used the position of the Sun and stars to tell them where they were. These included compasses, astrolabes and cross-staffs.

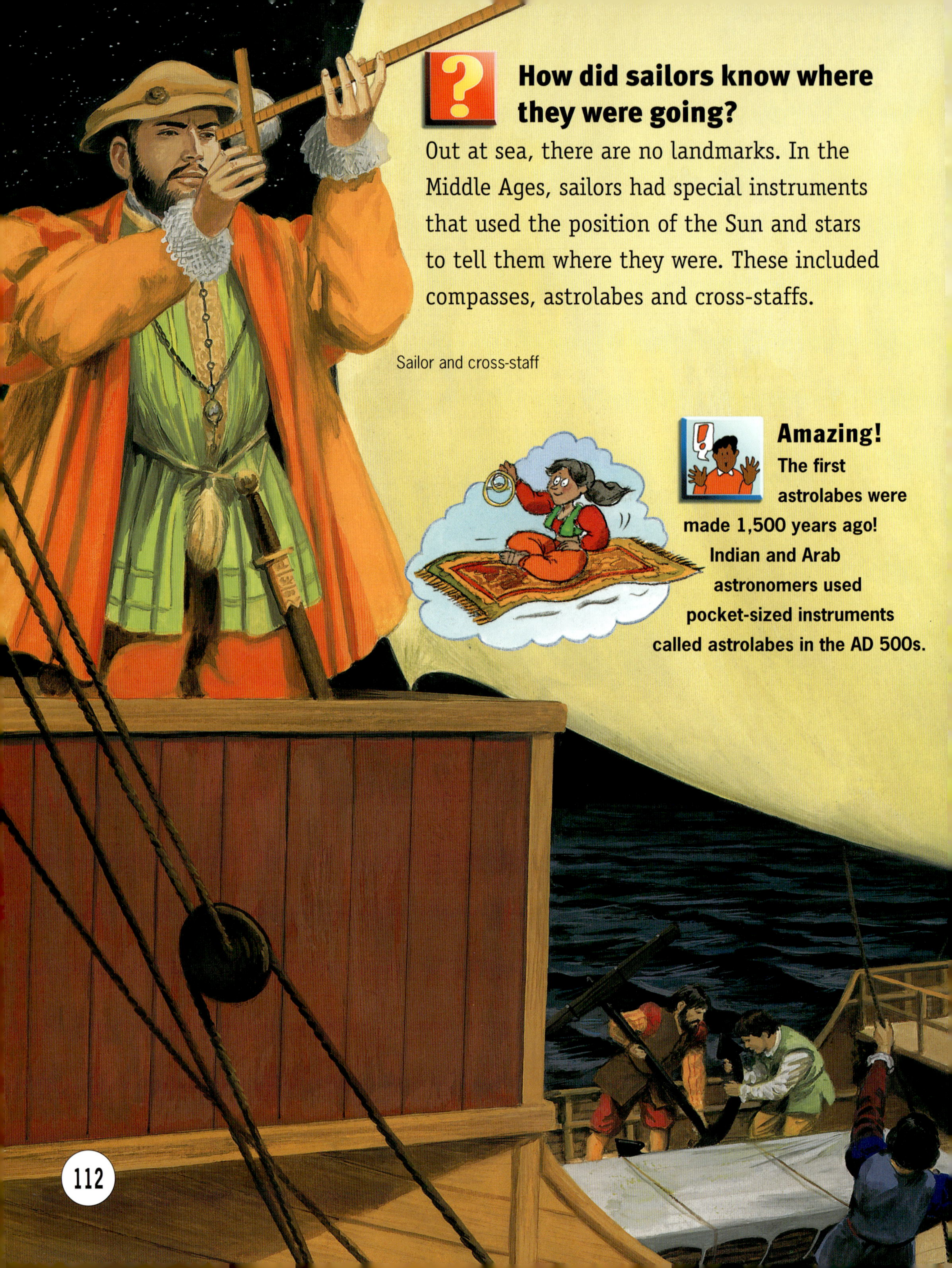

Sailor and cross-staff

Amazing!

The first astrolabes were made 1,500 years ago! Indian and Arab astronomers used pocket-sized instruments called astrolabes in the AD 500s.

Is it true?
Astrolabes only worked at night.

NO. You could use the position of the Sun instead of the stars, when you were sailing during the day. You looked at its position compared to the horizon.

How did an astrolabe work?

An astrolabe had two discs, one with a star map, and the other with measuring lines and a pointer. You compared them with the Sun or a star and the horizon to work out your position.

What is the pole star?

The only star which doesn't appear to move is above the North Pole. Sailors could tell where they were by looking at the pole star – it's lowest in the sky at the Equator.

Path of the stars with the pole star in the middle

Who made the first telescope?

Hans Lippershey, a Dutch man who made spectacles, probably made the first telescope in 1608. He noticed that if he put two lenses at different ends of a tube and looked through them, objects seemed to be nearer and clearer.

Is it true?

Newton saw a rainbow in his telescope.

YES. Isaac Newton noticed that the edges of objects seemed coloured when you looked through a telescope. That's how he began to work out that clear white light is made up of many different colours.

Hans Lippershey with his telescope

How does a telescope work?

The lens (curved piece of glass) at the front end of a telescope gathers light to make an image of an object that is far away. The lens at the back magnifies the image so it can be seen more clearly.

Simple cutaway of a telescope

Newton's reflecting telescope

Who put mirrors in a telescope?

Isaac Newton was the first person to make a mirror or reflecting telescope. He replaced the front lens with a dish-shaped mirror at the back. The mirror reflected the image on to a smaller mirror, and then into the eye.

Amazing! You can see Saturn's rings through a telescope. Telescopes magnify images (make them bigger) so much that you can even make out Saturn's faint rings – which are about 1.3 billion km away!

Nicolaus Copernicus

Who said that planets go round the Sun?

Nicolaus Copernicus explained this idea in a book in 1543. The problem was, the Church stated that God had put the Earth at the centre of the Universe. You could be put to death for saying that the Earth went round the Sun.

Who was put on trial for star-gazing?

Few scientists were brave enough to say that they agreed with Copernicus's findings that the Earth went round the Sun. The Italian astronomer Galileo was – and was put on trial for his ideas in 1634.

Galileo on trial

Is it true?
The Church accepted that Galileo was right in the end.

YES. The Church eventually agreed that the Earth and other planets travelled round the Sun. But they didn't do this until 1992 – 350 years after Galileo's death!

Who first used a telescope for astronomy?

Galileo started making telescopes in 1609, not long after Lippershey made his. Galileo was the first person to realize how useful a telescope would be for looking at the night sky. Because he could see more clearly, he made lots of important new finds, such as discovering four of Jupiter's moons.

Amazing! Copernicus explained the seasons. By showing that the Earth goes round the Sun and also spins at the same time, Copernicus explained why some times of the year are warmer than others.

Galileo looking at the night sky

Where do astronomers put their telescopes?

Observatories are buildings where astronomers go to look at the sky. They house the most powerful telescopes on Earth. The telescopes are usually kept in a room with a dome-shaped roof. Observatories have other instruments too, such as very precise clocks, to help keep accurate time and records.

Pulkovo Observatory, Russia

Where's the best place to build an observatory?

Where you'll get the clearest view! Most are built away from city lights. Mountain-tops are best of all, because they poke above any clouds that might spoil the view.

Is it true?

The Greenwich Observatory houses the most telescopes.

NO. The Kitt Peak National Observatory in Arizona, USA has the most optical telescopes. One of them, the Mayall Telescope, is 4 m across!

Amazing! The Ancient Babylonians used observatories. They did their star-gazing from stepped towers called ziggurats.

How can a telescope see through the roof?

It doesn't have to – an observatory's domed roof is specially designed to slide open at night, so that the picture through the telescope isn't distorted (blurred) by looking through a window. The telescope can be pointed at any place in the sky.

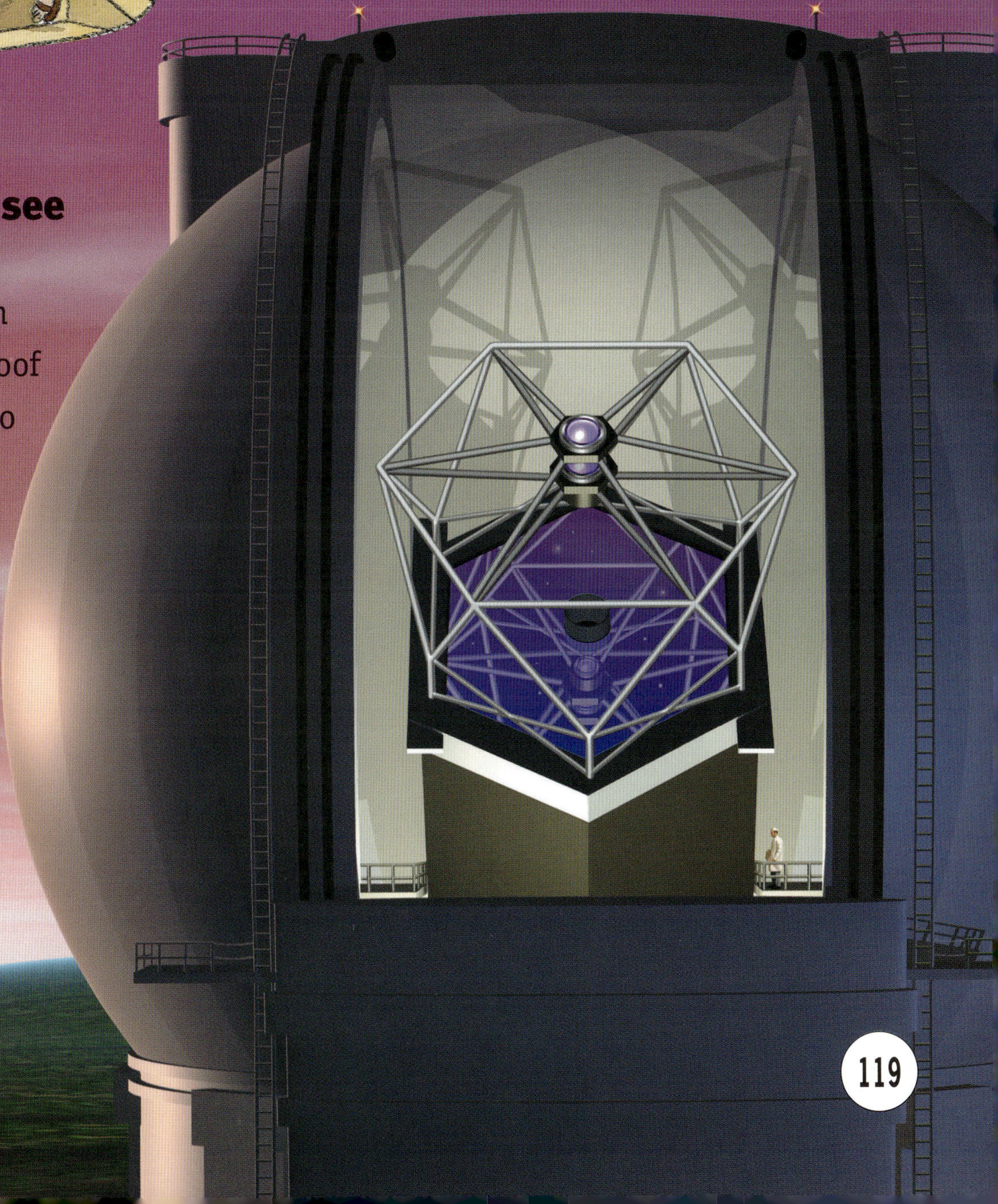

Telescope in a domed observatory

How deep is space?

Early astronomers thought that all the stars were the same distance from us, forming a simple shell around the Earth. Now we know that some stars are relatively close to us, and others are trillions of kilometres away.

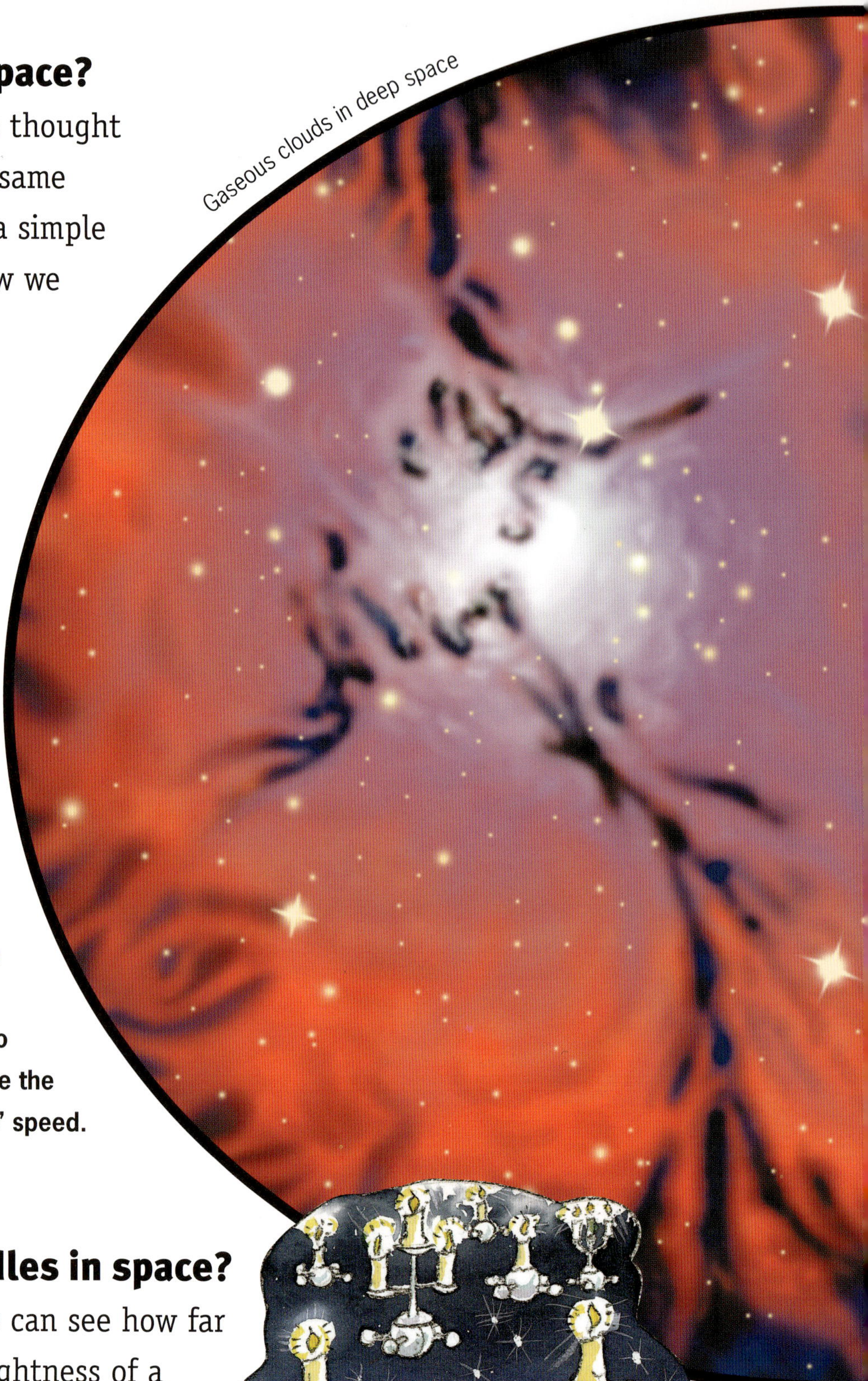
Gaseous clouds in deep space

Amazing!

Galaxies move so quickly they are different colours. The light waves from them change, just as a fire engine's siren sounds lower after it zooms past. We use the colour to measure the galaxies' speed.

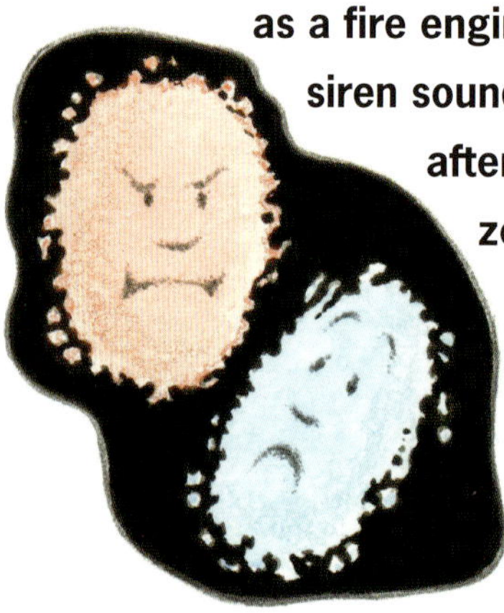

Are there candles in space?

Not really. But we can see how far away a galaxy is by the brightness of a special type of star, called a 'standard candle'. The further away the galaxy, the dimmer the candle.

How do you measure the distance to a star?

Watch the tip of your finger as you move it towards to your nose. The closer it gets, the more cross-eyed you become! Astronomers can tell the distance to a star by measuring how 'cross-eyed' a pair of telescopes has to be to see it.

Is it true?

We measure how far the stars are in kilometres.

NO. They're so far away, that we use light years instead. A light year is how far light travels in one year – 9,461 billion km!

Who made the first radio telescope?

Radio telescopes are like giant satellite dishes that pick up invisible radio waves and similar waves, instead of light rays. Unlike light, radio waves can travel through cloud, so radio telescopes can be built just about anywhere! An American called Grote Reber made the first one in the 1930s.

Reber's radio telescope was a simple metal frame

Amazing! A telescope can be 8,000 km long. The Very Long Baseline Array (VLBA) stretches across the USA. It has ten different dishes and produces the best-quality radio images of space from Earth yet!

Which are the most powerful radio telescopes?

The ones that are made up of several different radio dishes, such as the Very Large Array (VLA) in New Mexico, USA. The VLA has 27 dishes, each 25 metres across. Scientists compare the findings from all 27 dishes to get super-accurate results.

VLA, Socorro, New Mexico

Where is the biggest radio telescope?

The world's biggest single-dish radio telescope was built in Puerto Rico in the Caribbean nearly 50 years ago. It is 300 metres across – so it would take you more than ten minutes to walk around the edge of it.

Radio telescope, Puerto Rico

Is it true?

Only ten astronomers are allowed to use the VLA.

NO. It is used by over 500 astronomers a year.

Some study our near-neighbours in the Solar System, while others peer way beyond our galaxy to others in deepest space.

Gravity telescope

What's a gravity telescope?

A gravity telescope uses laser beams to measure its own length. As a gravity wave passes through Earth from space, it stretches the telescope by less than the width of an atom! Four huge gravity telescopes were built at the end of the 1990s.

Can we see black holes?

We can through a gravity telescope. Although light can't escape a black hole, gravity can. When a black hole swallows up a star, for example, there's a 'ripple' of gravity through space. Gravity wave telescopes spot the ripples.

A black hole

Amazing! The biggest gravity wave telescope is 4 km long! No one knows yet what new things gravity wave telescopes will help astronomers discover.

What's the weirdest telescope?

The Super Kamiokande telescope near Tokyo is just a big tank full of very pure water, buried deep underground. Very sensitive cameras detect teeny-weeny particles called neutrinos zooming through the Earth, by recording microscopic flashes of light in the water.

Is it true?

Neutrinos have a dark secret.

YES. Scientists think the Universe is full of something heavy, which they call dark matter. Neutrinos may be part of it!

Are there telescopes in space?

Yes – the first one went up in the 1960s. Space is a perfect place for looking at the stars. The sky is always dark and cloudless. Away from Earth's pollution and wobbly atmosphere, the stars shine steadily and brightly, instead of twinkling as they do to us on Earth.

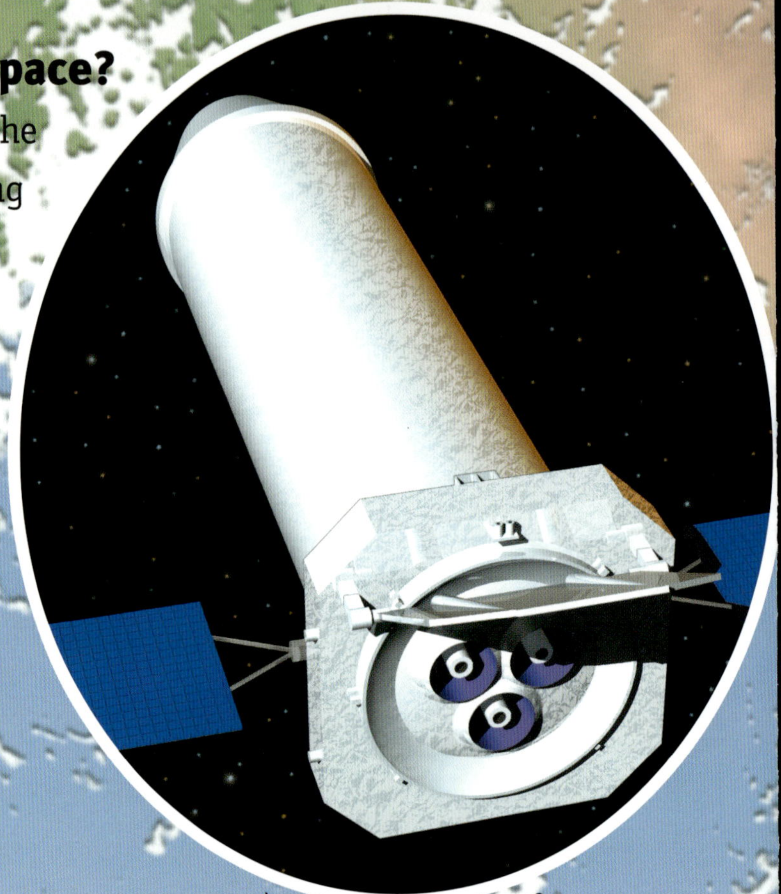

X-ray multi-mirror telescope

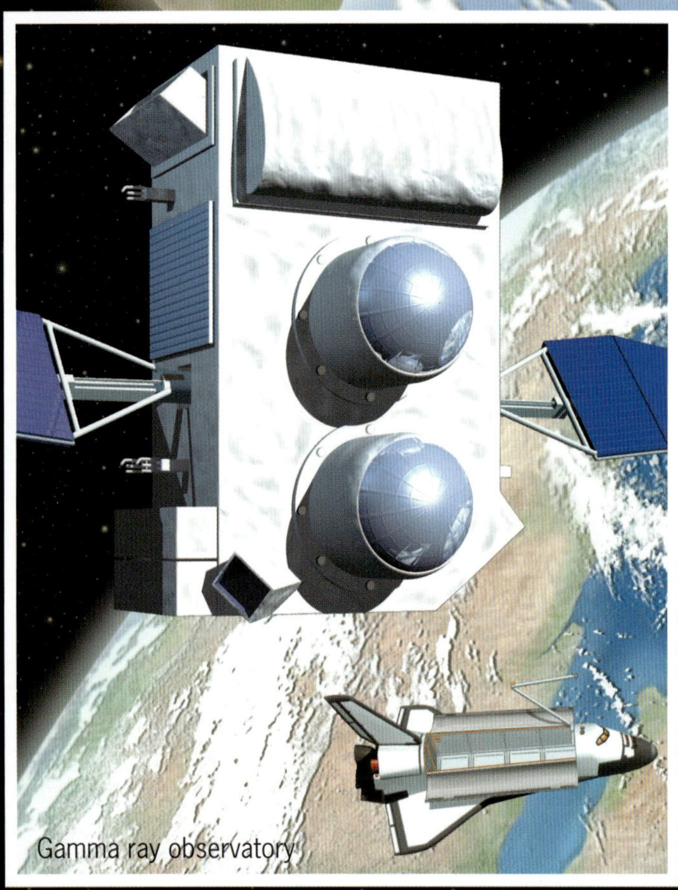

Gamma ray observatory

Are there observatories in space?

Yes – some observatories use powerful gamma rays, which can penetrate all the gas and dust in the galaxy, to show us what is happening in its centre. The Compton gamma ray observatory was launched into space by the shuttle.

Which telescope is in orbit?

The most famous is the Hubble Space Telescope, which was carried into orbit on the space shuttle Discovery in 1990. It circles the Earth every 90 minutes, about 600 km above us. It beams radio signals of information to astronomers on Earth.

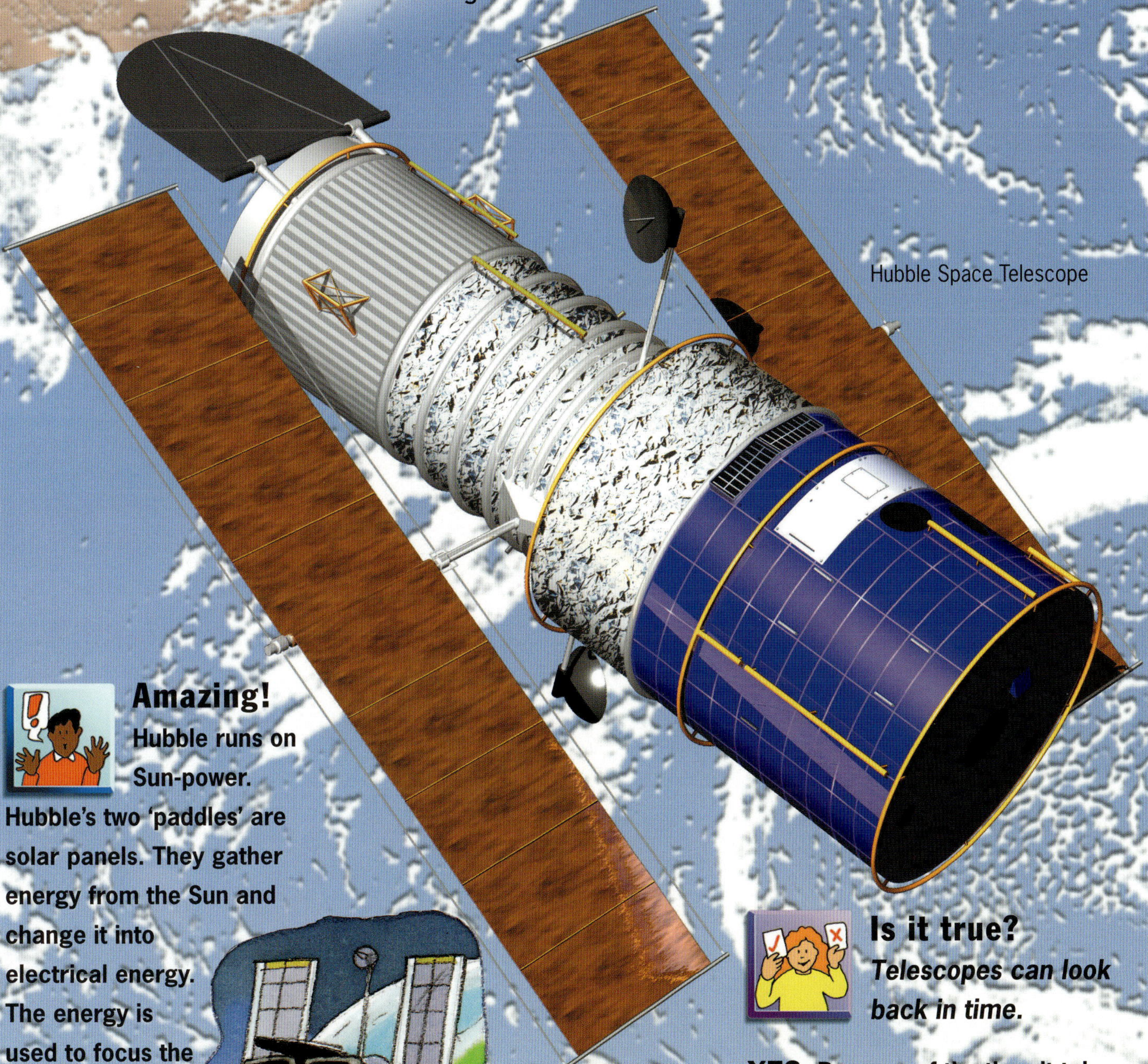

Hubble Space Telescope

Amazing!

Hubble runs on Sun-power. Hubble's two 'paddles' are solar panels. They gather energy from the Sun and change it into electrical energy. The energy is used to focus the telescope and beam data home.

Is it true?

Telescopes can look back in time.

YES. Because of the time it takes X-rays to travel through space, Chandra can see quasars as they were ten billion years ago!

What's better than a powerful telescope?

Seeing for yourself in close-up – but it's too dangerous and expensive to send astronomers deep into space. That's why space probes are such important tools. Space probes are fitted with cameras. They beam back close-up photos of faraway planets and comets.

Cassini-Huygens spacecraft

Amazing! Chandra is a billion times more powerful than the first X-ray telescope. If telescopes keep improving at this rate, we'll be able to see the farthest edges of the Universe in 30 years' time!

Is it true?
A probe found a watery world.

YES. The Voyager 2 probe photographed what might be water on Jupiter's moon, Europa. If there is life out there, probes will probably find it first.

VLA in space

Could we build Very Large Arrays in space?

Scientists are already testing a cluster of satellites that fly in perfect formation, using laser beams. The same technology will be used to create a string of small satellite telescopes, making one huge 'eye' in space.

Moon observatory of the future

Could we build an observatory on the Moon?

The dark side of the Moon would be a perfect site. Always pointing away from the Earth, it is shielded from man-made X-rays. But building there would be very expensive.

CHAPTER FIVE

PREHISTORIC LIFE ON EARTH

How old is the Earth?

Earth is millions and millions of years old. In fact, our planet is four-thousand-six-hundred-million years old. When the Earth's age (4.6 billion years) is written as a number, it looks like this: 4,600,000,000. It's hard for us to imagine anything so old.

Earth today

Amazing! **Some of Earth's oldest known rocks are found in Scotland. They are about 3.5 billion years old.**

Fiery conditions on Earth before life began

Has there always been life on the Earth?

Nothing at all lived on the Earth for the first billion (1,000 million) years of the planet's existence. The conditions were not right for life. There were no plants or animals of any kind. Earth was a dangerous place where life could not survive.

Has the Earth always looked the same?

These maps show how Earth's land and sea looked in the past. To fit everything on them, Earth has been drawn as an oval. For a long time, all land was joined together in one giant mass. Over millions of years it broke up into smaller pieces. They turned into today's continents.

200 million years ago

150 million years ago

80 million years ago

Is it true?

The continents are still moving.

YES. **The continents move about 4 centimetres each year – the length of your little finger. Millions of years in the future, Earth will look very different from today.**

When and where did life on Earth begin?

Life on Earth began about 3.5 billion years ago. The first life appeared in the sea. It was born into a world that looked very different from today. The atmosphere was filled with poisonous gases. The sky was pink, and the sea was rusty-red.

Conditions on Earth were hostile when life first began

Is it true?
Earth is the only planet with life on it.

MAYBE. This is one of the greatest unsolved mysteries. Life probably does exist on other planets besides Earth, but nothing has been found so far. The search continues.

Beginnings of life

How did life begin?

It is thought that life began when lightning hit the sea. Lightning sent energy into the water. Chemicals in the sea were mixed together by energy. New substances, called amino acids, were made, from which life was able to grow.

Amazing! **The first living things on Earth were so small you could fit thousands of them on the head of a pin.**

Close-up of bacteria

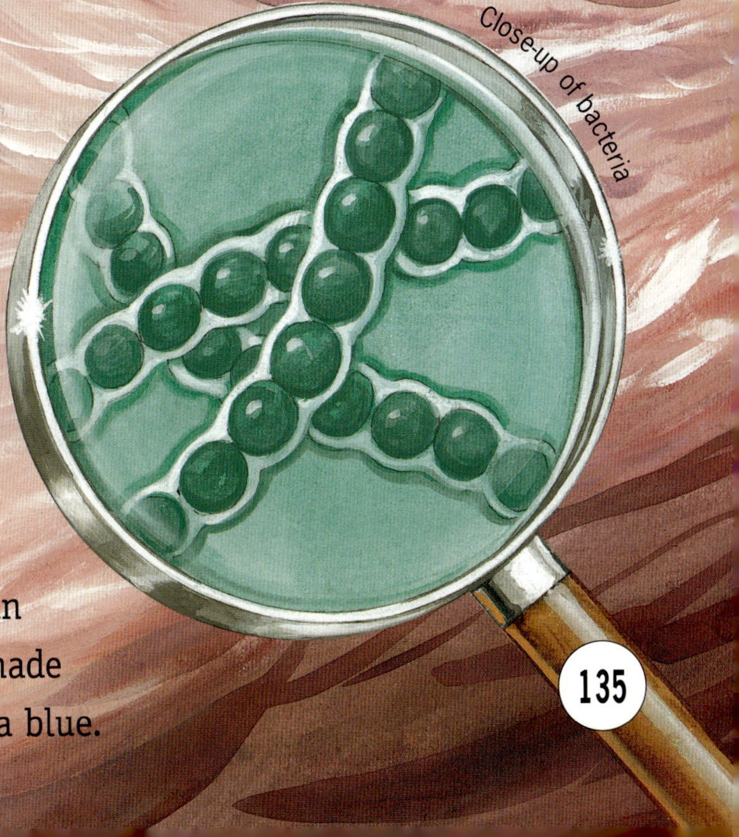

What were the first living things?

The first living things were bacteria. They lived in the sea. Some bacteria changed into algae, which were simple plants. Algae lived in the sea in masses, like huge blankets. They made oxygen, which helped to turn the sky and sea blue.

Early sea life

Which animals lived in the sea?

For millions of years all life lived in the sea. It was home to a huge variety of creatures, such as shellfish, worms, sponges and jellyfish. None of these animals had backbones.

Cladoselache (an early shark)

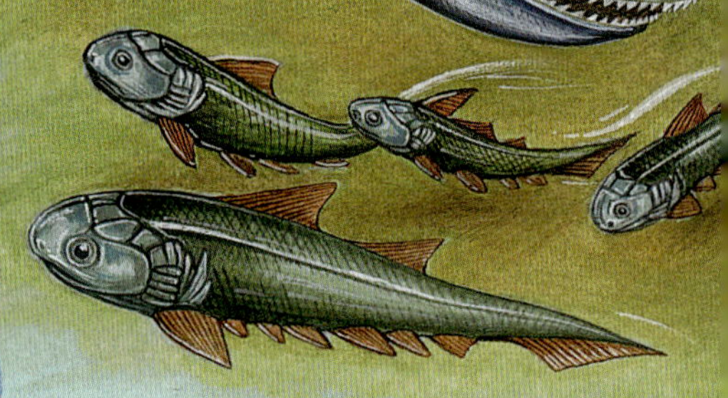

Acanthodians

Is it true?

The very first fish didn't have jaws.

YES. Instead of jaws to open and close their mouths the very first fish sucked food into their mouths. They are called jawless fish.

Heliobatis fossil

Which animals first had backbones?

About 510 million years ago, new kinds of animals appeared in the sea. They were the first fish, and they were the first animals with backbones. Because they had backbones to support their bodies they could become much larger.

Amazing! In the Indian Ocean is a fish called a coelacanth. It has hardly changed for 350 million years. It is a living fossil.

What were early fish like?

Giant sharks, much larger than any alive today, swam through the oceans. They hunted smaller fish. Armoured fish grew bony plates to protect their soft bodies. Other fish had bodies covered in sharp spines.

When did life first appear on land?

About 440 million years ago, the first life appeared on land. It was simple plant life, similar to today's mosses. Then, about 400 million years ago, the first land animals – worms, spiders, scorpions and insects – evolved as they moved on to the land.

Is it true?

There are no amphibians alive today.

NO. There are many different amphibians in the world today. Frogs, toads and salamanders are all amphibians.

Why did some fish grow legs?

Some fish began to live in shallow water. It was difficult to swim in the shallows. To help these fish move around they grew short legs. Some of them also grew lungs, which meant they could breathe air. These animals could live in water and on land.

Acanthostega (an early amphibian)

Amazing! **The lungfish is one of today's fish that can live out of water. It can breathe air.**

Which animal lives in water and on land?

An animal that can live in water and on land is called an amphibian. It means 'double life'. The first amphibians appeared by 350 million years ago. Gradually, they spent more and more time on land.

Ichthyostega
(an early amphibian)

What are reptiles?

About 300 million years ago, some amphibians changed into reptiles. They could live on land all the time. Reptiles have backbones and scaly skin, and most lay eggs. Many reptiles, such as crocodiles, spend lots of time in the water, but they can't breathe underwater. They use the Sun to keep their bodies warm.

Is it true?

Some early reptiles had sails on their backs.

YES. Dimetrodon had a skin 'sail' on its back. It soaked up the Sun's heat, and controlled the animal's body temperature.

Hylonomus

What did reptiles eat?

The first reptiles, such as Hylonomus, were small lizard-like animals that ate tiny creatures. Reptiles learned how to run quickly so they could catch fast-moving insects. As reptiles became larger, they caught and ate bigger prey, including other reptiles. Some reptiles only ate plants.

Amazing!

A small animal found in Scotland, in rocks that are 350 million years old, might be one of the first reptiles. But some scientists say it was an amphibian.

Hylonomus and dragonfly

Which reptiles had fur?

Some prehistoric reptiles grew fur on their bodies to keep themselves warm. These were the cynodonts. They lived about 245 million years ago. Over time they changed into a completely new group of animals, called mammals.

Cynognathus (a cynodont)

Thrinaxodon (a cynodont)

What were dinosaurs?

Dinosaurs were members of the reptile family. They first appeared about 225 million years ago. For 160 million years dinosaurs ruled the Earth. They walked on straight legs, tucked underneath their bodies, and they lived on land. The word dinosaur means 'terrible lizard'.

Is it true?

All dinosaurs were big.

NO. The tiny Compsognathus was about the same size as a chicken.

What did dinosaurs eat?

Some dinosaurs were carnivores. This means they ate meat and fish. Some were herbivores. These dinosaurs ate plants. A third group were omnivores. They had a mixed diet and ate both meat and plants. Some dinosaurs swallowed stones, which crushed food inside their stomachs so it was easier to digest.

Seismosaurus (a plant-eater)

Amazing! When Ankylosaurus filled its bony plates with blood it could have blushed pink!

Tyrannosaurus rex and Hypsilophodons

What colour were dinosaurs?

No one knows what colour dinosaurs were. Perhaps some had skins that matched their surroundings, making them hard to see. Some might have had bright markings to attract mates, or scare others away.

Could dinosaurs make noises?

Dinosaurs had voice boxes, which means they could make noises. Parasaurolophus had a long, hollow bone on top of its head. Perhaps it forced air through the bone to make a deep, hooting sound.

Amazing! **A dinosaur has gone into space! In January 1998, a fossil Coelophysis skull travelled on board the space shuttle Endeavour. The 220-million-year-old fossil flew four million miles around the Earth.**

Did dinosaurs care for their young?

Yes, some did. Maiasaura, whose name means 'good mother lizard', cared for its young. Parents looked after them until they were old enough to take care of themselves.

Maiasaura adult and young

Is it true?

Every animal on Earth died out with the dinosaurs.

NO. Lots of animals survived. Birds, mammals, amphibians, insects, small reptiles (lizards), fish, spiders, snails and crocodiles all lived.

Why did dinosaurs die out?

Dinosaurs died out 65 million years ago. Many people think this was because a big meteorite (a space rock) hit the Earth. It sent dust into the air which blotted out the Sun. Dinosaurs died because they were too cold and hungry.

Meteorite hitting Earth

Which creatures flew in the sky?

At the same time as dinosaurs walked on the land, other reptiles flew in the sky and swam in the sea. The sky reptiles were pterosaurs, which means 'winged lizards'. Their wings were not made from feathers, like a bird's, but from stretched skin.

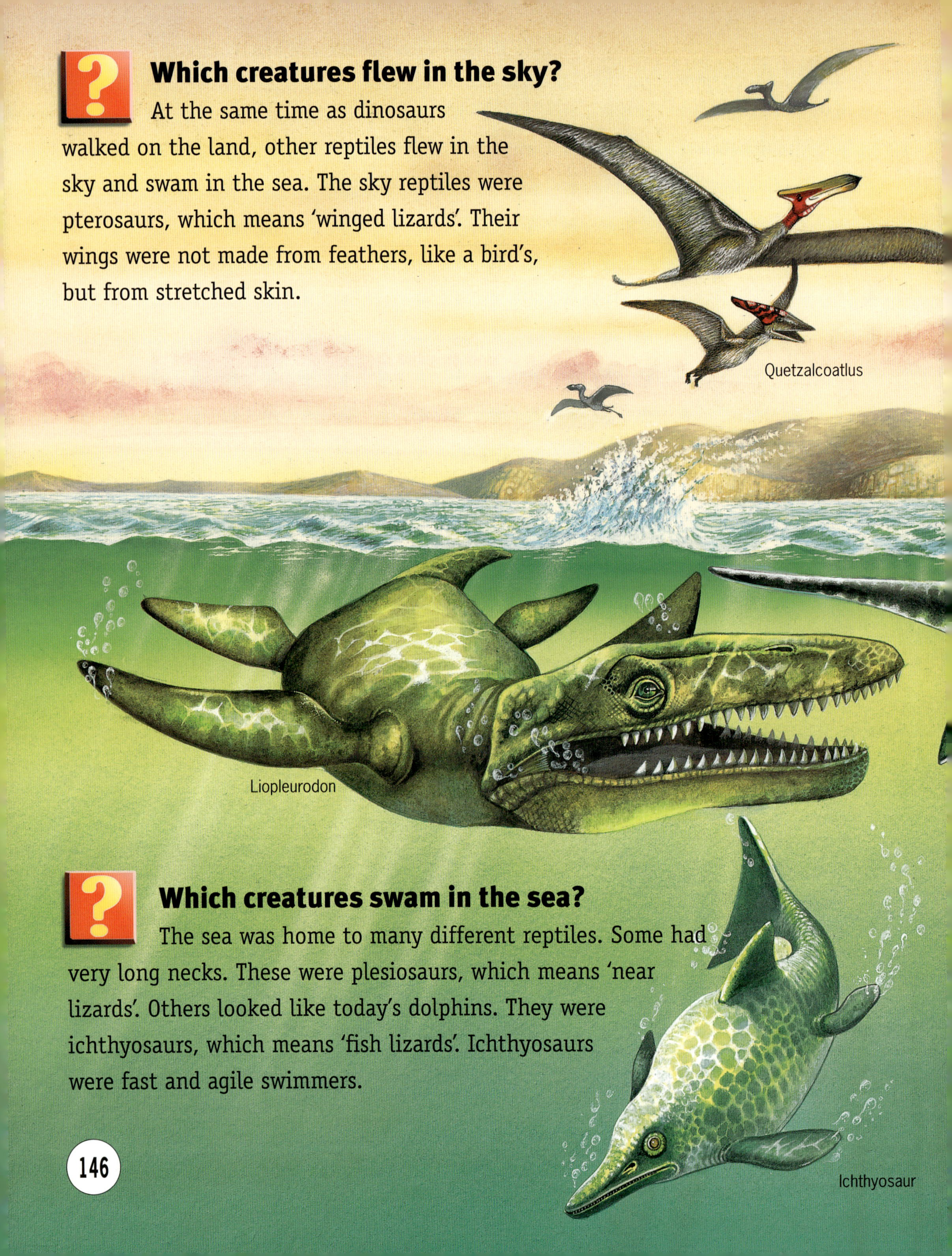

Which creatures swam in the sea?

The sea was home to many different reptiles. Some had very long necks. These were plesiosaurs, which means 'near lizards'. Others looked like today's dolphins. They were ichthyosaurs, which means 'fish lizards'. Ichthyosaurs were fast and agile swimmers.

Is it true?

One pterosaur was as big as a small plane.

YES. Quetzalcoatlus was an enormous pterosaur. It had wings 12 metres across. It is the biggest flying creature ever.

What did pterosaurs eat?

Some pterosaurs ate fish, which they scooped from the sea with their long beaks. Some pterosaurs may have held lots of fish inside their cheek pouches, as pelicans do today.

Feeding pterosaur

Amazing! The short-necked plesiosaur Liopleurodon grew to 23 metres and weighed 50 tonnes. It was a giant sea monster!

What are birds?

Birds are animals with backbones, they lay eggs, can make their own body heat, and have wings. They are also the only animals with feathers. Not all birds can fly. The first birds lived at the same time as the dinosaurs.

Is it true?

Ostrich eggs are the biggest eggs ever laid by a bird.

NO. The extinct bird Aepyornis laid the biggest eggs of all time. Each one was about the size of 150 hen's eggs.

Where do birds come from?

Birds evolved from small, meat-eating dinosaurs. Fossils show that some of these dinosaurs had feathers. They are called 'dinobirds'. The first 'dinobirds' probably could not fly.

Caudipteryx

Amazing! Today's hoatzin bird, which lives in South America, has claws on its wings when young – just like Archaeopteryx, its prehistoric ancestor, did.

Fossilized Archaeopteryx

Archaeopteryx

Which was the first true bird?

The first true bird – a bird that could fly – appeared about 150 million years ago. It is known as Archaeopteryx, which means 'ancient wing'. It had claws on its wings.

What are mammals?

Mammals have backbones, their bodies are covered in hair or bristles, they make their own body heat, and they feed their young on milk. They have larger brains than most other animals.

Early mammals

When did the first mammals appear?

The first mammals appeared on Earth about 220 million years ago. They lived at the same time as the dinosaurs. Mammals survived after the dinosaurs died out, and then they became the ruling animals on Earth. There are about 4,200 different kinds of mammals alive today.

Did mammals only live on land?

Mammals came to live in all of Earth's habitats. Many lived on land, but some, such as bats, were able to glide through the air on wings of skin. Other mammals swam in the sea, such as whales, dolphins and seals.

Basilosaurus

Amazing!

Woolly mammoths were big elephants with extra-long tusks up to 3 metres long. Their bodies were covered in fur.

Tyrannosaurus rex

Is it true?

The elephant is the largest land mammal ever to have lived.

NO. Indricotherium was the largest land mammal. It was almost 8 metres tall and as heavy as four elephants.

Amazing! One Australopithecus is called Lucy. Her bones were found in 1974, when a song with the name Lucy in it was on the radio. She was named after it.

A group of human ancestors collecting fruit

Australopithecus skull

Who were our ancestors?

Our earliest ancestors were apes that walked upright on two legs. Australopithecus, meaning 'southern ape', was one of the first apes to walk upright. It lived at least three million years ago, and was short and hairy.

Is it true?
Lucy was very short.

YES. Compared with a modern human, an adult Australopithecus like Lucy was very short – about 1.2 metres tall.

How did they live?

Australopithecus probably lived in small family groups. These bands of human ancestors wandered across the grassy plains of their homeland. They ate fruit, leaves, seeds and roots. They may have used sticks to help dig for food, and may have eaten meat, too.

Australopithecus finds

Where did they live?

Australopithecus lived in Africa. Bones of this upright ape have been found in several countries, including Tanzania, Ethiopia and South Africa. Africa is where human species probably began, a few million years ago.

Who were the very first humans?

The first people we think of as humans appeared in Africa. About two million years ago, Homo habilis (handy man) appeared. Then, more than one million years ago, Homo erectus (upright man) appeared, but they weren't modern humans.

Amazing!

Homo erectus had fire. Fire provided warmth, gave heat for cooking, and offered protection from predators.

Did they have any tools?

Homo habilis was the first tool-user. This is why he is called 'handy man'. He made simple tools, such as choppers, from pebbles. The tools made by Homo erectus were better. He shaped stones into hand axes, and he was the first to use fire.

What did they eat?

Homo habilis and Homo erectus ate meat and plants. Meat probably came from dead animals which they found. They may have hunted for some small animals. Plants gave them berries and leaves. They used stone tools to cut and scrape their food.

Is it true?

***Homo erectus* was a wanderer.**

YES. More than one million years ago, Homo erectus began to move out of Africa, travelling to Europe and Asia.

Homo erectus people hunted and gathered their food

When did modern humans appear?

Just over 100,000 years ago Homo sapiens appeared. The name means 'wise man'. They were modern humans. In Europe they lived during the freezing Ice Age, a time when glaciers covered the land. The Ice Age ended 12,000 years ago.

Mammoth hunt

Is it true?

Homo sapiens have all died out.

NO. All people on Earth today are members of Homo sapiens. If they had died out, like other kinds of early human, none of us would be here today!

Where did they live?

Homo sapiens first appeared in Africa, and from there, they spread out across the world. They lived in cave entrances, and in places sheltered by overhanging rocks. In the open they made huts from branches, covered with skins.

As the climate grew warmer, Homo sapiens people migrated across the world

Amazing! People who lived during the Ice Age played musical instruments. They made whistles from bones, and drums from shoulder-blades.

Animal carving

Cave painting

Were they artists?

The humans who lived in Europe during the Ice Age were among the first artists. They painted pictures of horses, bison and deer on the walls of their caves. Bone and ivory were carved into figures of animals and people.

How do we know about life in the past?

We find out about life in the past by looking for evidence. Fossils are one kind of evidence. They are the remains of living things that have been preserved. Objects made by humans, such as stone tools, are another kind of evidence.

A collection of fossils

Is it true?

Plants can't be fossilized.

NO. Plants can become fossils, in the same way that animals can. By studying them we learn about the plants that once grew on Earth.

1

2

3

4

How is a fossil made?

It takes millions of years to make a fossil. The pictures on the left show how it happens. (1) An animal dies. Its body sinks to the bottom of a lake. (2) Sand and silt cover its body. (3) The flesh rots away. Minerals seep into the bones and turn them to stone. The animal is now a fossil. (4) The fossil is found.

Who looks for prehistoric life?

People who look for remains of prehistoric animals, such as dinosaurs, are called palaeontologists. People who look for ancient humans are archaeologists. They find great things, such as bones, tools, buildings, jewellery and weapons.

Palaeontologists excavating fossilized dinosaur bones

Amazing! A sticky resin that oozed from pine trees trapped insects that landed on it. It hardened into a substance called amber. Prehistoric insects are perfectly preserved inside it.

CHAPTER SIX

EXPLORING EARTH

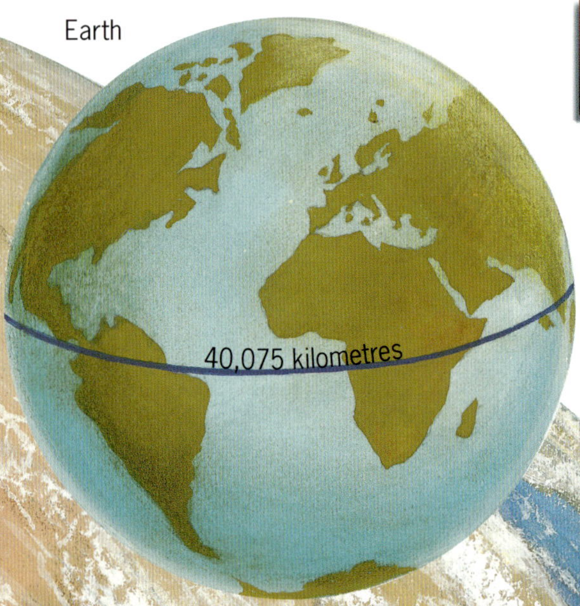

How big is the Earth?

The Earth is shaped like a gigantic ball, slightly squashed at the top and bottom. Around its middle, where it's fattest, it measures 40,075 kilometres. It would take you almost a year to walk right round the Earth, without a rest.

What's inside the Earth?

The Earth is made up of layers of rock and metal. We live on the hard, rocky surface, called the crust. Below, the layers are so hot that they've melted and turned runny. The centre of the Earth is a ball of almost solid metal.

Amazing! People used to think the Earth was flat. If they sailed too far in one direction, they thought they'd fall off the edge!

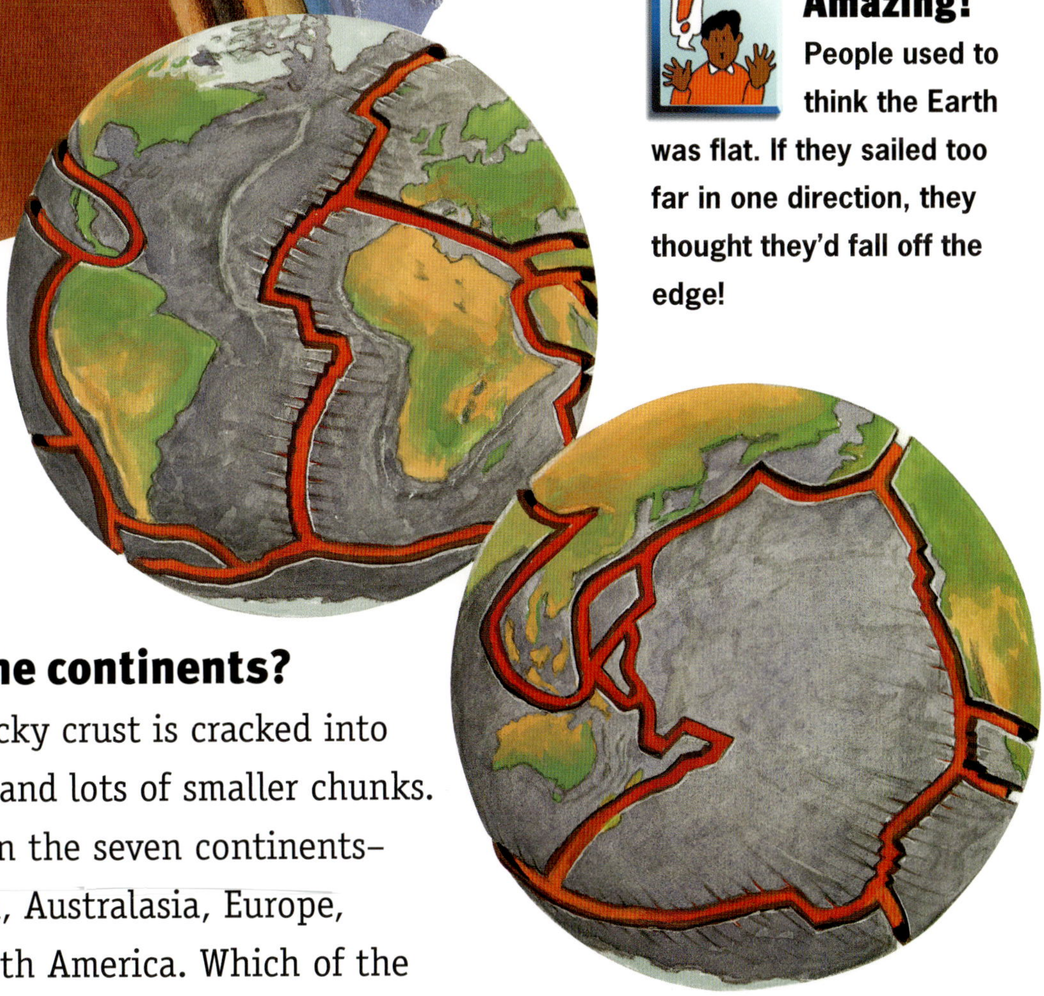

Earth's main continental plates

What are the continents?

The Earth's rocky crust is cracked into several gigantic pieces and lots of smaller chunks. The large pieces contain the seven continents– Africa, Antarctica, Asia, Australasia, Europe, North America and South America. Which of the continents do you live on?

How are caves carved out?

Deep down beneath many mountains is a secret world of tunnels and caves. Caves are carved out by rainwater trickling through cracks in the ground. As the rain falls, it mixes with gas in the air and soil. It turns into a weak acid which eats away at the rock.

Amazing! The tallest stalagmite in the world grows in a cave in Slovakia. It's 32 metres high – that's as tall as 17 people.

Mammoth Caves, Kentucky, USA

Where are the longest caves?

The Mammoth Caves in Kentucky are the longest caves on Earth. They stretch for 560 kilometres. The biggest single cave is the Sarawak Chamber in Malaysia. Its floor is the size of 30 soccer pitches.

Prehistoric cave art

Which caves are art galleries?

Thousands of years ago, prehistoric people sheltered in caves, and painted pictures on the walls. The best art gallery is in the Lascaux Caves in France. The walls are covered with hundreds of animals, including bison and mammoths.

Limestone cave system

Is it true?
Potholers are people who explore caves.

YES. Even though it's wet, cold and dark underground. The deepest a potholer has ever been is 1,508 metres in a cave in Russia.

How are mountains built?

Some mountains are built when two pieces of the Earth's crust bump or crash into each other. The rock in between is pushed up into giant fold mountains. Other mountains are made when huge blocks of rocks are squeezed up.

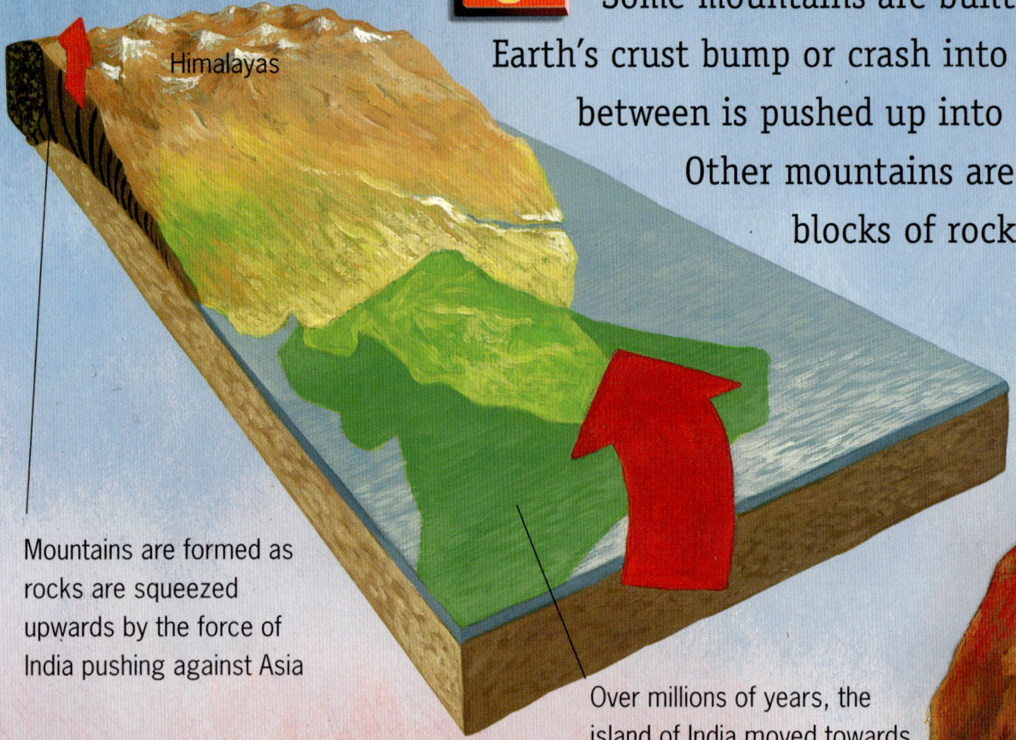

Amazing! **The first people to climb to the top of Mt Everest were Sherpa Tenzing Norgay and Edmund Hillary in 1953.**

Shrinking mountain

Why are mountains shrinking?

It takes millions of years for mountains to grow. But many are shrinking every day. Mountains are being worn away by wind, frost and ice, which attack the peaks and break off chips of rock.

Where are the highest mountains?

The highest mountains in the world are the Himalayas in Asia. This massive mountain range has 12 of the world's 14 highest peaks, including Mt Everest. At 8,848 metres, it's the highest mountain on Earth.

Is it true?

The higher up a mountain you go, the hotter it gets.

NO. The higher you go, the colder it gets. That's why the tops of some peaks are capped in snow – and why many mountain animals have warm, winter coats.

Where are the Poles?

The North and South Poles are at either end of the Earth. The North Pole is surrounded by the frozen Arctic Ocean. The South Pole is in the middle of icy Antarctica.

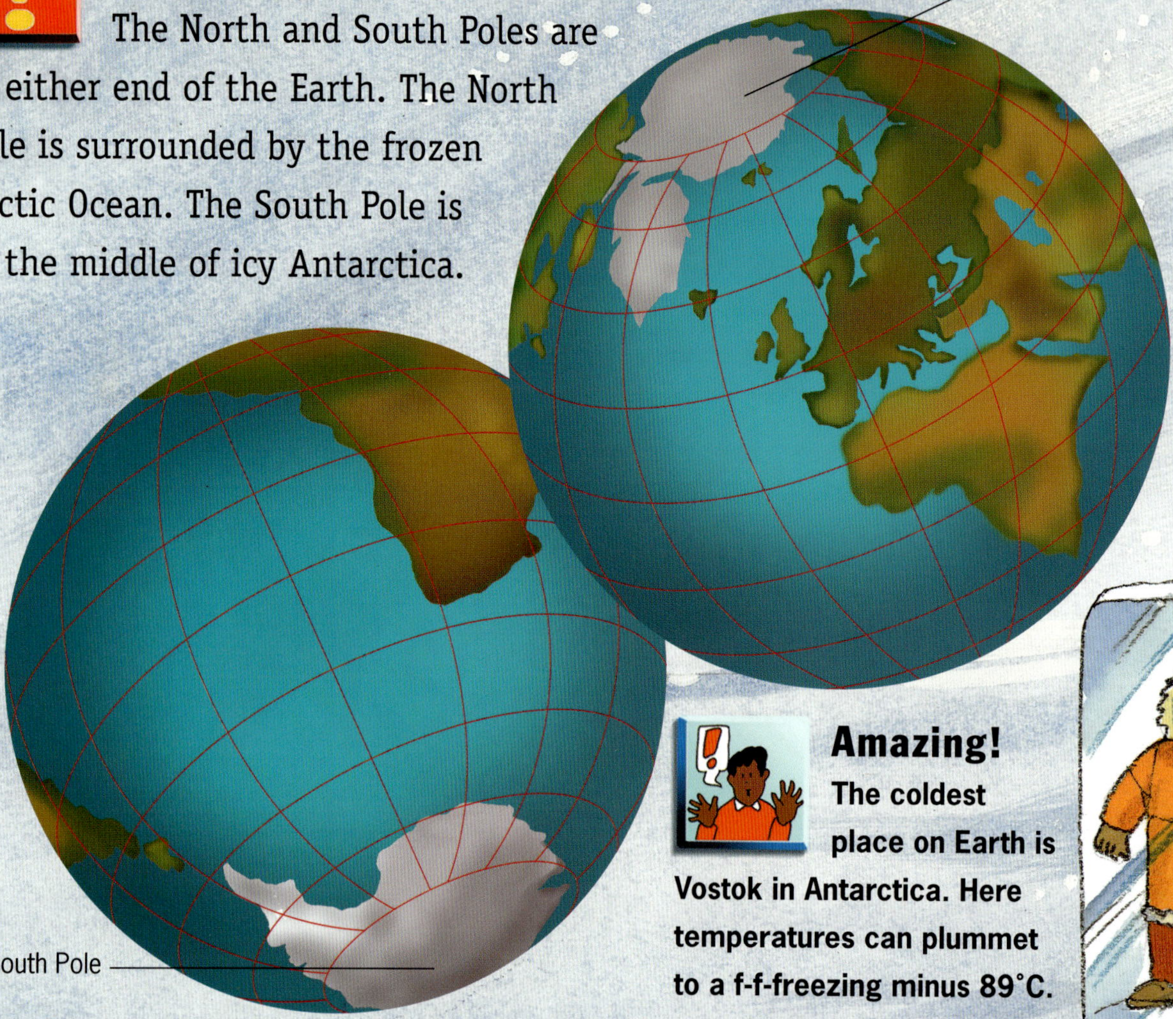

Amazing!

The coldest place on Earth is Vostok in Antarctica. Here temperatures can plummet to a f-f-freezing minus 89°C.

Why are the Poles cold?

The Poles are the coldest places on Earth. They're battered by blizzards and covered in ice and snow. The Poles are cold because the Sun's rays hit them at a slant, so they're spread out and very weak.

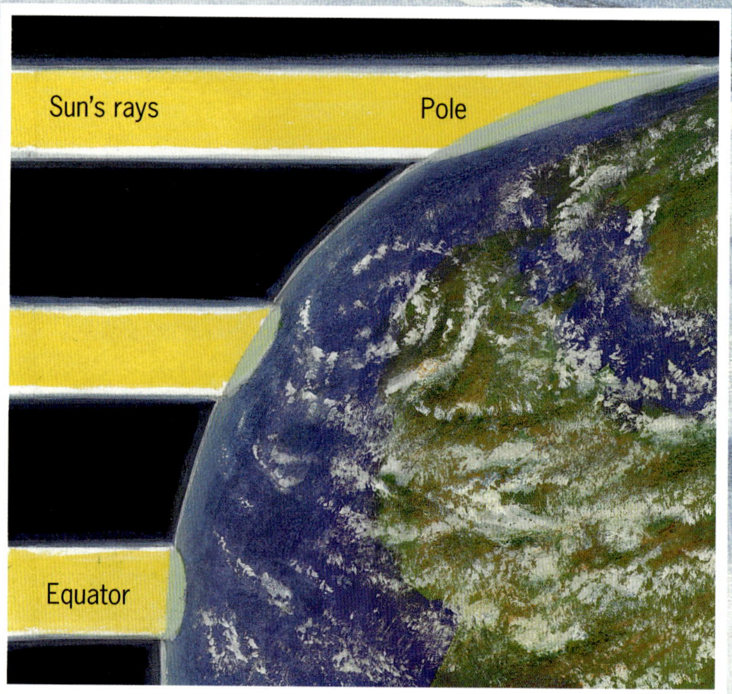

Is it true?

Penguins live at the North Pole.

NO. Penguins only live around the South Pole. But you might bump into a polar bear at the North Pole.

Who reached the South Pole first?

The first person to reach the South Pole was Norwegian explorer Roald Amundsen in December 1911. He beat the British team of Captain Scott by about a month. Exhausted and suffering from frostbite, Scott died on the way home.

Captain Scott in the Antarctic

Amazing! In 1912, the luxury liner, Titanic, hit an iceberg and sank in the North Atlantic. It was on its maiden (first) voyage from Southampton to New York.

Iceberg seen from underwater

What are icebergs?

Icebergs are giant chunks of ice that break off the ends of glaciers and drift out to sea. Only about a tenth of an iceberg shows above water. The rest is hidden under the sea. This makes them very dangerous to passing ships and boats.

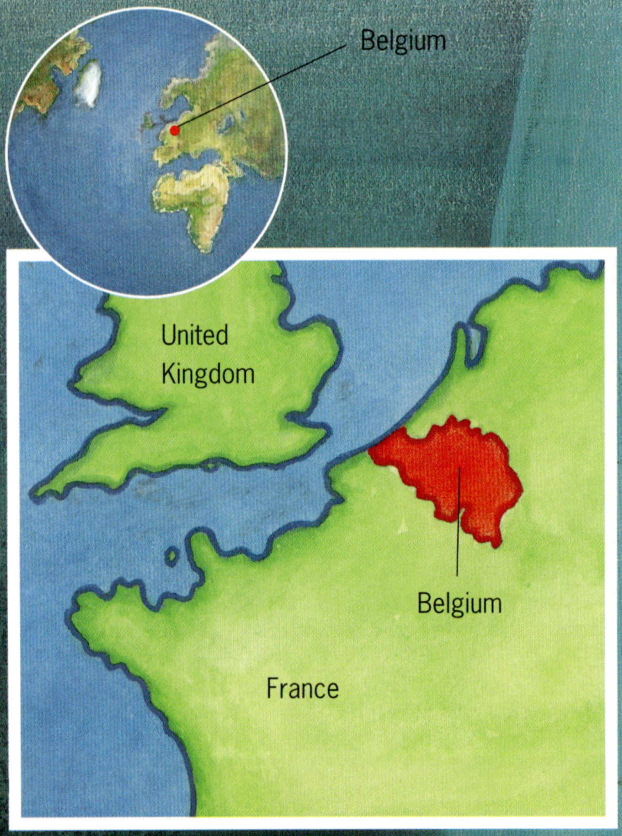

Which was the biggest iceberg?

The biggest iceberg ever was seen near Antarctica. It was about the size of Belgium! The tallest iceberg was more than half as high as the Eiffel Tower in Paris.

Is it true?
Baby icebergs are called calves.

YES. A baby iceberg breaking off a glacier is called 'calving'. Even smaller icebergs are called 'bergy bits'.

Which is the longest glacier?

Glaciers are enormous rivers of ice that flow slowly down a mountainside. The Lambert-Fisher Glacier in Antarctica is over 600 kilometres long. It's the longest glacier in the world. About a tenth of the Earth is covered in icy glaciers.

Why does the sea flow in and out?

Twice a day, the sea washes on to the shore at high tide. Then it flows back out again at low tide. The tides are caused by the Moon and Sun pulling the sea into giant bulges on either side of the Earth.

Amazing!

If all the coasts were straightened out, they'd stretch round the Earth 13 times. At 90,000 kilometres, Canada has the longest coast.

Why are beaches sandy?

Sand is made from tiny fragments of rock and shells, crushed up by the wind and water. Sand is usually yellow or white. But some sand is black because it contains volcanic rock or coal.

How are cliffs carved out?

Along the coast, the rocks are worn away by the force of the waves. As the waves crash against the shore, they carve out cliffs, caves and high arches. Sometimes an arch collapses, leaving a stack, or pillar, of rock.

Is it true?

White horses swim in the sea.

YES. **But they're not real horses. They're the white, foamy tops of the waves as they gallop towards the shore.**

How big is the sea?

The sea is absolutely huge! Salty sea water covers about two-thirds of our planet so there's far more sea than land. The sea lies in five oceans – the Pacific, Atlantic, Indian, Arctic and Southern Oceans.

Amazing! **The first person to set sail around the world was Ferdinand Magellan. He set off from Spain in 1519. Magellan died but one of his ships made it back three years later.**

Which is the biggest ocean?

By far the biggest ocean is the vast Pacific. It alone covers a third of the Earth. At its widest point, between Panama and Malaysia, it stretches almost halfway around the world.

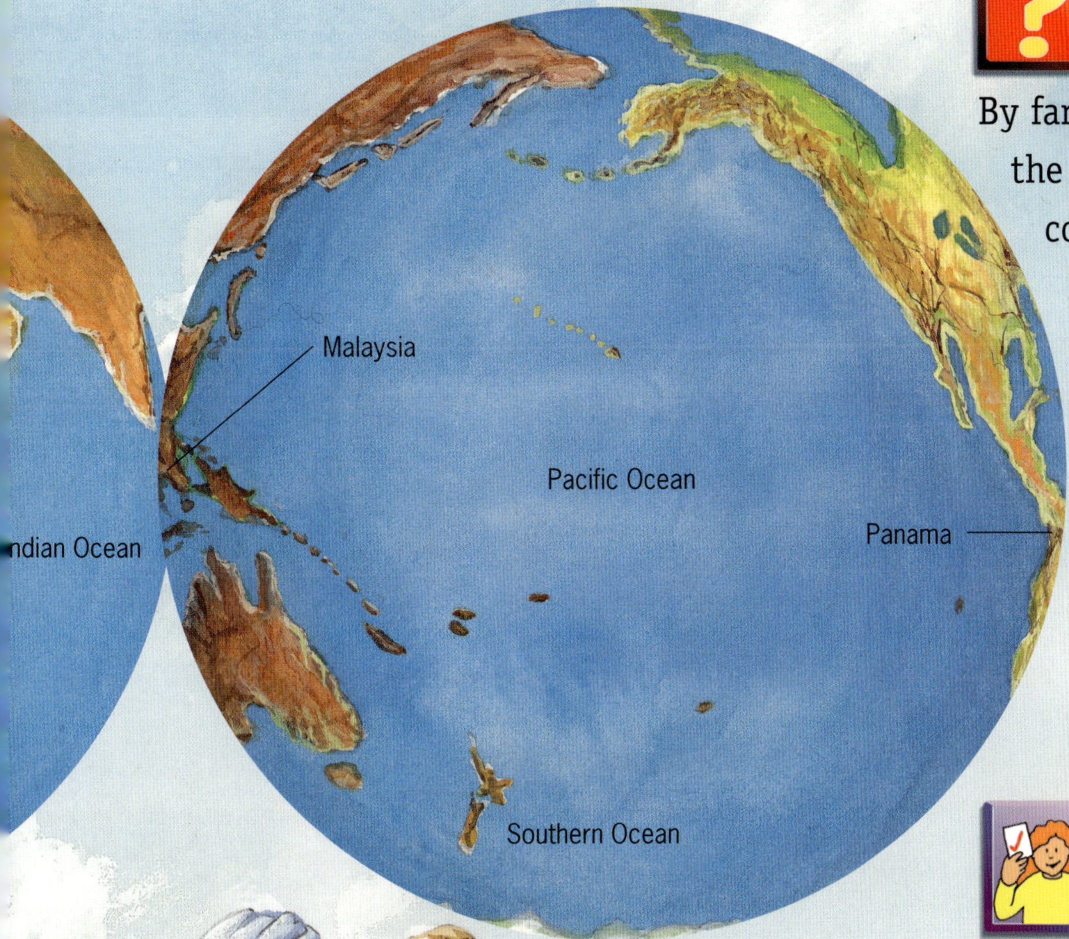

Is it true?

The Arctic is the warmest ocean.

NO. The Arctic's the coldest ocean of all. For most of the year, it's covered in ice.

Why is the sea salty?

The sea's salty taste comes from ordinary salt. It's the same stuff you sprinkle on your food. The rain washes the salt out of rocks on land, then rivers carry it into the sea. The people in the picture are collecting salt left after sea water dries.

Is the sea bed flat?

No, it isn't. There are mountains, volcanoes and valleys on the sea bed, just as there are on land. The Mid-Atlantic Ridge is a long line of undersea mountains in the Atlantic Ocean. Steep underwater valleys are known as trenches.

Is it true?
Deep-sea fish use torches.

YES. It's pitch black in the deep sea. Some fish make their own lights so they can see in the dark.

Amazing! The highest mountain on Earth from base to peak isn't Mt Everest. It's Mauna Kea in the Pacific. This huge, underwater mountain is 10,203 metres tall. Its top pokes out above the sea to make an island in Hawaii.

Who builds coral reefs?

Huge coral reefs are built by tiny sea creatures called polyps. The polyps build hard, stony cases around their soft bodies. When they die, the cases are left behind. Millions and millions make a coral reef.

Coral reef

Who dived the deepest?

In 1960, two scientists dived nearly 11 kilometres into the Marianas Trench in the Pacific Ocean. This is the deepest dive ever made. They travelled in a small submersible called Trieste. It took almost five hours to reach the bottom.

Where do rivers begin?

Rivers begin as fast-flowing streams high up on mountainsides. Some streams bubble up from underground. Others flow from lakes or trickle from the tips of icy glaciers when they start to melt. The start of a river is called its source.

Amazing! **The world's shortest river is D River in Oregon, USA. It's a tiny 37 metres long.**

Is the Nile or the Amazon the longest river?

The Nile in Egypt is the longest river on Earth. It flows for 6,695 kilometres. The Amazon in South America is just 295 kilometres shorter.

Angel Falls

How high are waterfalls?

The highest waterfall in the world is Angel Falls in Venezuela. It plunges 979 metres down the side of a mountain. Angel Falls are 20 times higher than the famous Niagara Falls in North America.

Is it true?
Rivers flow into the sea.

YES. Most rivers flow into the sea at their deltas. But some rivers flow into lakes and a few flow into deserts.

Which lake is the biggest?

The biggest freshwater lake on Earth is Lake Superior in North America. It covers 82,350 square kilometres. That's almost as big as Austria. Lake Superior is one of five huge lakes called the Great Lakes.

Is it true?

There's a monster in Loch Ness.

MAYBE. Some people say Nessie is a type of prehistoric reptile that lives in the lake. Others say this is nonsense. What do you think?

Amazing! The Dead Sea in the Middle East is so salty that you can float on the surface. No fish can live in it.

Where is the highest lake?

Lake Titicaca in South America is the highest lake on which boats can sail. It's 3,810 metres up in the Andes Mountains. People who live around the lake build boats from lake reeds.

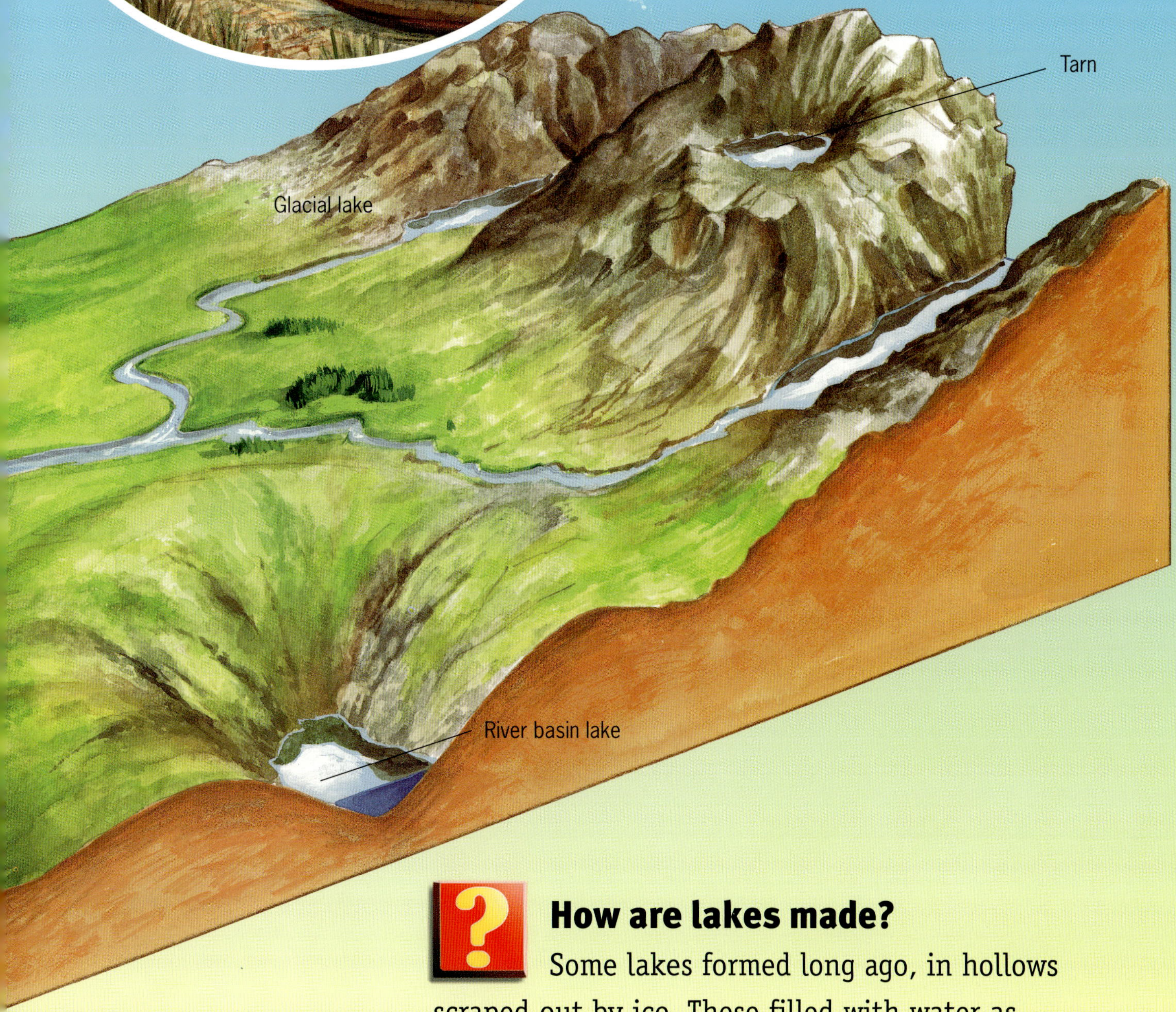

How are lakes made?

Some lakes formed long ago, in hollows scraped out by ice. These filled with water as the ice melted. Some lakes form in the tops of volcanoes or when a river cuts through a bend.

What is a coral island?

A coral island began life as a coral reef growing around the top of an underwater volcano which stuck out from the sea. When the volcano sank into the sea, it left a horseshoe or ring-shaped coral island behind.

Amazing!

If you lived on the island of Tristan da Cunha in the South Atlantic, your nearest neighbours would be almost 2,500 kilometres away.

Where is the biggest island?

An island is a chunk of land with water all around it. The biggest island is Greenland, in the icy Arctic Ocean. It measures more than 2 million square kilometres. Australia is bigger than that, but it usually counts as a continent.

Which country has most islands?

The country of Indonesia in South East Asia is made up of more than 13,000 islands. But many of the islands are tiny and people only live on about 1,500 of them.

Is it true?

New islands keep being made.

YES. In 1963, a new island, called Surtsey, burst out of the sea near Iceland when an undersea volcano erupted.

Why are deserts dry?

Deserts are the driest places on Earth. In some deserts it doesn't rain for years at a time. In others, it never rains at all. Some deserts are also scorching hot. In the daytime, the sand's hot enough to fry an egg on.

Amazing! The Sahara Desert is the biggest, sandiest desert in the world. It covers about a third of Africa.

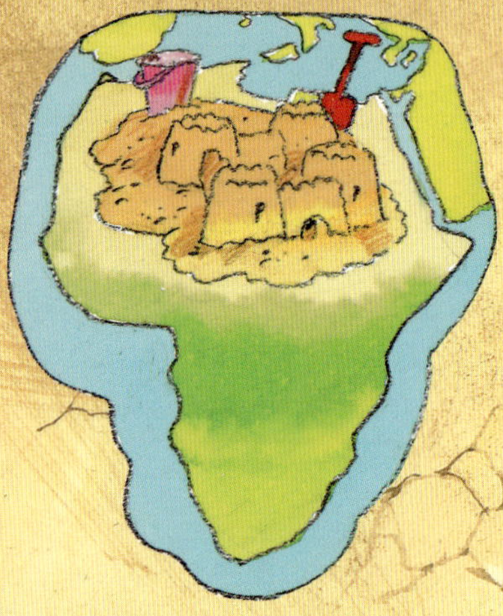

Sandy desert seen from above

Can sand dunes move?

Strong winds blowing across the desert pile the sand up into giant heaps, or dunes. The biggest stand 200 metres tall. The dunes creep forward every year and can bury whole desert villages.

Sand dunes covering a town

Are all deserts sandy?

No, they're not. Only about a quarter of all deserts are sandy. Most deserts are rocky or covered in gravel and stones. Some deserts have high mountains or strange-shaped rocks towering up from the ground.

Is it true?
Mushrooms grow in the desert.

YES. Well, mushroom-shaped rocks. They're carved into shape by sand blown by the wind, like a giant piece of sandpaper.

Why are rainforests so wet?

Because it rains almost every single day! Late most afternoons, the sky goes black and there's a heavy thunderstorm. Rainforests grow along the equator where it's hot and sticky all year round. It's the perfect weather for plants to grow.

Rainforest

Where do the biggest forests grow?

The biggest forests in the world stretch for thousands of kilometres across the north of Europe and Asia. The trees that grow here are conifers. They're trees with needle-like leaves and cones.

Is it true?

The paper we use comes from forests.

YES. You could make more than 1,500 copies of this book from a single conifer tree.

Amazing!

The biggest rainforest grows in South America along the banks of the River Amazon. It's home to millions of plants and animals.

How do rainforests grow?

Rainforests grow in layers depending on the height of the trees. The tallest trees poke out above the forest. Below them is a thick roof of tree-tops called the canopy. Next comes a layer of shorter trees, herbs and shrubs.

African savannah (grassland)

What are grasslands?

Grasslands are huge plains of grass, trees and bushes. They grow in warm, dry places where there's too little rain for forests to grow, but enough rain to stop the land turning into a desert.

South American gauchos farming on grassland

Why did a grassland turn to dust?

In the 1930s, farmers in the south-west USA ploughed up the grasslands to grow wheat. But a terrible drought turned the soil to dry, useless dust which blew away in the wind. This was called a dustbowl.

Dustbowl

Amazing! **Grassland animals eat different bits of the grass to avoid competition – zebras eat the tops, wildebeest eat the stems.**

What are grasslands used for?

People use grasslands for grazing animals such as cattle which are raised for their meat. They also grow crops such as wheat and barley in gigantic fields. One wheat field in Canada was the size of 20,000 soccer pitches.

Is it true?
Rice is a type of grass.

YES. Rice is a cereal plant, which belongs to the grass family. The grains of rice come from the flower-heads. Rice grows in flooded fields in South East Asia.

CHAPTER SEVEN

VIOLENT EARTH

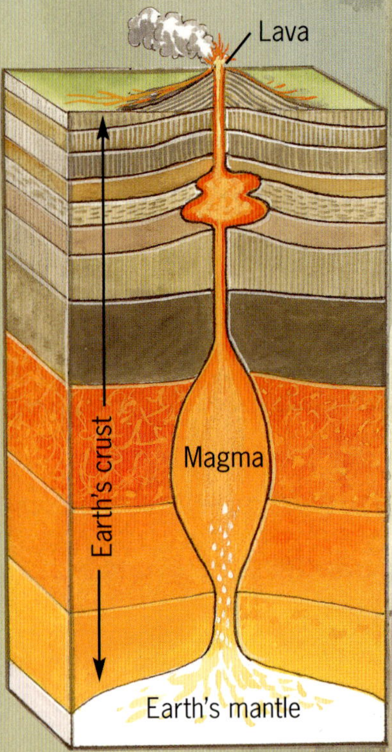

Why do volcanoes blow their tops?

Volcanoes are mountains that spit fire. Deep under the Earth there is red-hot, runny rock called magma. Sometimes the magma bursts up through a crack in the Earth's crust and a volcano erupts.

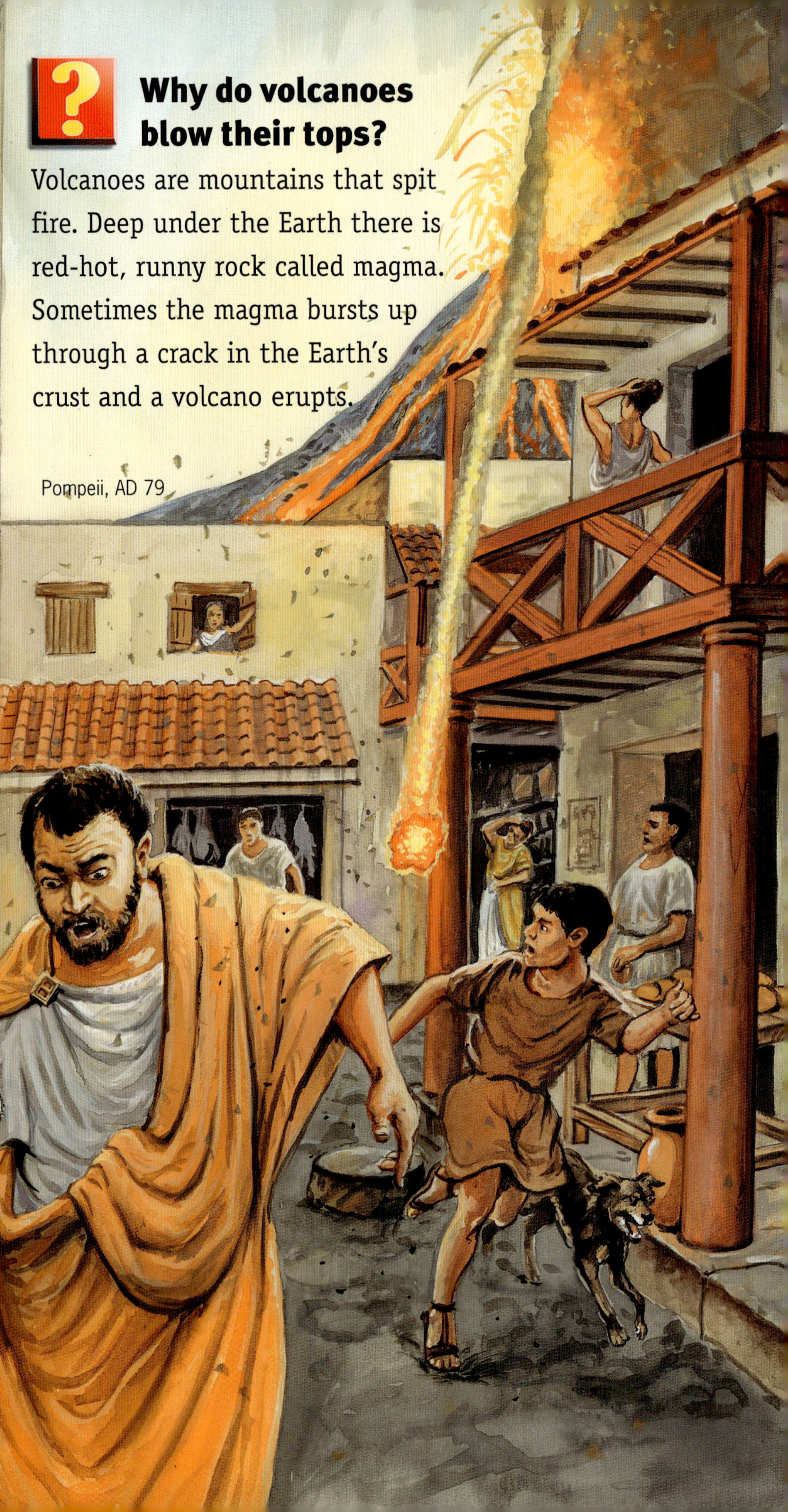

Pompeii, AD 79

Amazing! Some of the world's highest mountains are volcanoes. They include Mt Kilimanjaro in Africa. Luckily for this nosy lion, Kilimanjaro is now long extinct.

What is lava?

Once magma has erupted from a volcano, it is called lava. Some lava is thick and lumpy. Some is thin and runny. In the air, it cools and turns into hard, black rock.

Is it true?

Volcanic ash can flow as fast as a train.

YES. Clouds of gas and ash can flow across the ground at over 160 kph!

What happened to Pompeii?

In AD 79, Mt Vesuvius in Italy blew its top in a massive explosion. The nearby city of Pompeii was buried under a huge cloud of hot ash and rock. Thousands of people were suffocated. Others fled for their lives.

Mt St Helen's, USA was a dormant volcano that erupted

How long do volcanoes sleep for?

Hundreds or even thousands of years. A sleeping volcano is called dormant, but it can wake up at any minute. A volcano that still erupts is called active. An extinct volcano is one that is never likely to erupt again.

Geyser in Yellowstone Park, USA

Amazing! **The most active volcano on Earth is Kilauea in Hawaii. It has erupted non-stop for almost 20 years! All that lava means the island of Hawaii is getting bigger, every day.**

Why do people live near volcanoes?

Despite the danger, many people all over the world live near volcanoes. The ash that explodes out of a volcano makes the soil very rich for growing crops. People also use volcanic rock for building.

Town covered in ash after eruption of Mt Pinatubo, Philippines

Is it true?

You only get volcanoes on land.

NO. There are hundreds of volcanoes on land and many more under the sea. Some poke out above the surface to form islands, such as Hawaii.

Why do geysers gush?

Geysers are giant jets of scalding water and steam. They happen in places with lots of volcanoes. The red-hot rocks underground heat water far below the surface until it's so hot it shoots through a crack.

What makes the Earth shake?

The Earth's surface is cracked into enormous pieces which drift on the red-hot, runny rock below. Sometimes two pieces push and shove each other, making the Earth shake.

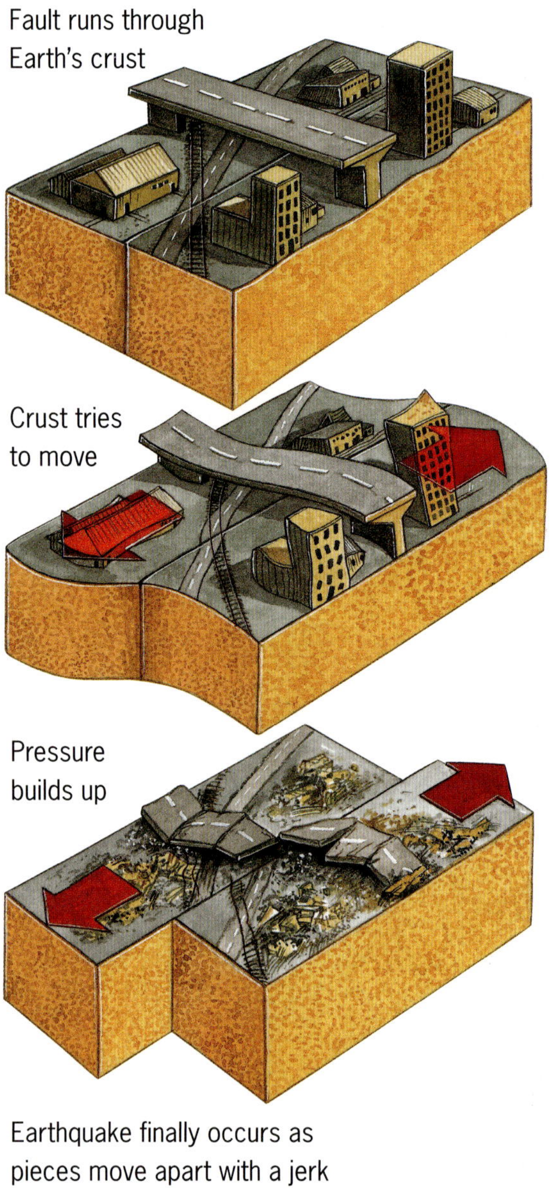

Kobe earthquake, Japan, 1995

How much damage do earthquakes cause?

Big earthquakes do lots of damage. Huge cracks open up in the ground. Houses, roads and bridges shake and fall down. In the worst earthquakes, many people are killed and injured by buildings that collapse on top of them.

How do scientists measure an earthquake?

An earthquake sends shock waves rippling through the ground. Scientists study these waves to see how big the earthquake is. They measure earthquakes on a scale of 1 to 10. Each quake on the scale is 30 times worse than the one before.

Seismograph (earthquake measuring device)

Is it true?
People used to think earthquakes were caused by fish.

YES. In Japan, people thought quakes were caused by a giant catfish wriggling about on the sea bed. The gods had to put a rock on the fish's head to make it stay still!

What is a tsunami?

Tsunamis are gigantic waves which can be 30 metres high and 200 kilometres long. The word tsunami means 'harbour wave' in Japanese because of the way the waves crash into the harbour. They are also called tidal waves.

Is it true?

The biggest tsunami was as tall as the Statue of Liberty.

YES. This colossal wave was 85 metres high, almost as tall as the Statue of Liberty. It swept past Japan in 1971.

Amazing!

A tsunami can travel across the sea at high speed. Some race along at 900 kph. That's as fast as a jet plane. The deeper the water, the faster they flow.

How do tsunamis start?

Tsunamis are triggered off by volcanoes or earthquakes under the sea. At first, the waves are low as they speed across the sea. As they reach land, the water piles up into a massive wave which crashes down on to the shore.

Tsunamis can leave boats stranded inland

What happens when a tsunami hits land?

When a tsunami hits land, watch out! It smashes down on to the shore, washing houses, people and boats away. A tsunami can sweep a boat into the air and dump it far away.

How do floods happen?

Many floods happen when it rains very heavily and rivers overflow. They burst their banks and flood the land all around. You also get floods in stormy weather when high tides or gigantic waves sweep on to the shore.

Amazing! The Thames Barrier was finished in 1984 to stop the River Thames flooding and drowning London. Ten huge steel gates swing up to make a massive dam.

Flash flood of Ouvèze River, France

What are flash floods?

Flash floods are floods which happen very suddenly, with no warning. Sometimes there isn't time to evacuate buildings in the flood's path. Flash floods can happen in the desert too, during a rare downpour of rain.

River Nile in flood

Are some floods useful?

Yes, they are. The River Nile in Egypt used to flood every year, leaving rich mud on the fields. The mud made the soil ideal for farmers to grow bumper crops. The Nile doesn't flood any more because a large dam was built to store its water.

The Mississippi River, USA, flooded 80,000 square kilometres, in 1993

Is it true?

Floods can wash whole buildings away.

YES. In 1955, a flood in the USA washed a four-storey wooden hotel clean away. Imagine how surprised the guests were when they looked out of their windows!

When do thunderstorms happen?

Thunderstorms usually happen on a hot, summer's day when the air is warm and sticky. Watch out for huge, dark, tall thunderclouds gathering in the sky. They're a sure sign a storm's brewing. Time to head indoors!

What makes thunder rumble?

Lightning is incredibly hot, about five times hotter than the Sun's surface. As it streaks through the sky, it heats the air so quickly that it makes a loud booming sound. This is the sound of thunder.

Where do thunderstorms begin?

Thunder starts in cumulonimbus clouds. They turn the sky purply black and blue. Some of these clouds are massive. The tallest can grow 18 kilometres high. That's more than twice the height of Mt Everest.

Is it true?

Lightning happens before thunder.

NO. They happen at exactly the same time. But you see lightning before you hear thunder because light travels more quickly than sound.

Cumulonimbus thundercloud

Amazing! The Vikings believed that thunder was caused by the bad-tempered god, Thor, hurling his hammer across the sky.

What makes lightning flash?

Inside a thundercloud, strong winds hurl droplets of water around. They bump and bash into each other. This makes the cloud crackle with static electricity which builds up and suddenly streaks through the sky as lightning. Lightning can flash inside clouds or from cloud to ground.

Amazing!

Park ranger, Roy C. Sullivan, was struck by lightning a record seven times. He suffered burns, singed hair and eyebrows, and he even lost his toenails!

Empire State Building, New York City, during thunderstorm

Does lightning ever strike twice?

Yes, it does. The Empire State Building is struck about 500 times a year! Many tall buildings, such as churches and skyscrapers, have lightning conductors to carry the electricity of the lightning safely away.

There are many stories of ball lightning entering houses

What is ball lightning?

Lightning comes in different shapes, such as forked, sheet and ribbon lightning. Ball lightning looks like a ball of fire. People have seen balls of lightning float into their house, then explode with a bang.

Is it true?

Lightning takes the slowest path to the ground.

NO. **It takes the quickest. That's why you should never shelter under a tall tree during a storm. If the lightning strikes the tree, you might get fried.**

Where do avalanches strike?

Avalanches strike on snow-covered mountainsides. A huge slab of snow and ice suddenly breaks loose and crashes downhill. Avalanches can slide at speeds of up to 320 kph, as fast as a racing car, as hundreds of tonnes of snow hurtle down the slope.

Sniffer dogs search for buried victims

Can people survive avalanches?

Avalanches are deadly. They can bury people, cars and whole villages in their path. Victims suffocate under the snow unless they're rescued quickly. Rescue teams use specially trained dogs to sniff survivors out.

Amazing! In World War I, soldiers fighting each other in the Alps used avalanches as weapons. They fired guns at the mountainsides to set off killer avalanches.

Is it true?
Yodelling can set off an avalanche.

YES. In some Swiss mountain villages yodelling is banned in spring in case it sets an avalanche off. You're not allowed to shout or sing loudly either, in case the vibrations of sound waves in the air shake and loosen the snow, to start an avalanche.

What sets off an avalanche?

If the snow gets too heavy, it can suddenly start to slip and slide. But other things can trigger an avalanche. A skier, or even a car door being slammed, can set the snow sliding.

Layers of snow and ice build up on mountainside

Weight of snow creates cracks, and a large chunk slips away

Why are blizzards dangerous?

A blizzard is a snowstorm. Strong winds blow the snow into drifts and it can be difficult to see. A blizzard can bring a busy city to a standstill. People and traffic can't move about, and schools and offices have to be closed.

Amazing! You don't only get snow in cold places. In 1981, snow fell in the Kalahari Desert in Africa for the first time in living memory. The temperature dropped to a chilly minus 5°C.

Which is the snowiest place?

The snowiest place in the world is Mt Rainier in Washington, USA. In one year, snow 30 metres deep fell there. That's enough snow to build a snowman as tall as 17 people. Fancy having a go?

What is a hailstone made from?

A hailstone is a small ball of ice that starts life in a thundercloud. Inside the cloud, a chip of ice is tossed up and down many times. It gets coated in layers of ice, just like the layers of an onion.

Build-up of a hailstone within a thundercloud

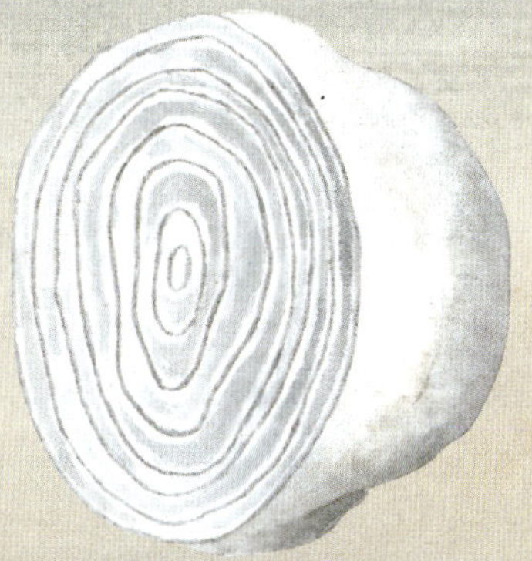

Cutaway of a hailstone, showing the layers of ice

Is it true?

The biggest hailstone was the size of a peach.

NO. It was bigger than that! Hailstones are usually the size of peas but the biggest was the size of a watermelon. It fell in Kansas, USA, in 1970.

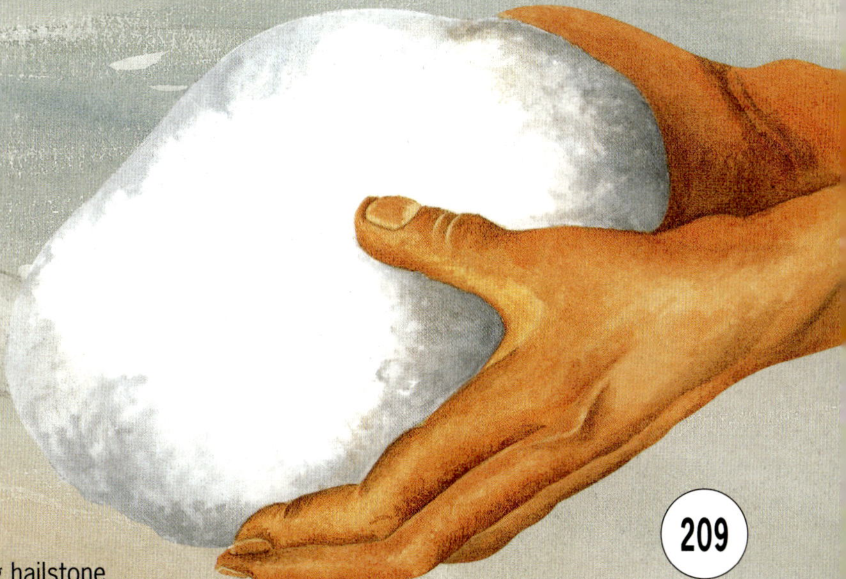

Record-breaking hailstone

What are hurricanes?

Hurricanes are giant storms that begin over warm tropical seas. They are like huge spinning wheels of wind, rain and clouds. They sweep across the sea, then begin to die down when they reach land.

Is it true?

Hurricanes have names.

YES. Hurricanes are given names from an alphabetical list. A new list is made every year. The names of the worst hurricanes, like Andrew or Carol, are never used again.

How big are hurricanes?

Hurricanes can be enormous. Some measure 3,000 kilometres across and even the smallest are about half the size of Britain. Winds inside a hurricane can blow at over 300 kph.

Hurricanes can even pick up and dump aeroplanes

Amazing!

If you could collect the energy inside a hurricane for one day and turn it into electricity, it would run the whole USA for six months.

An Atlantic hurricane hits the island of Antigua

Eye of hurricane seen from space

Do hurricanes have eyes?

Yes, they do. The eye is a patch of calm, clear weather in the hurricane's centre. As the eye passes over land, there's a break in the storm for an hour or so. Then it begins again.

What makes a tornado twist?

A tornado is a fierce, twisting wind which hangs from a thundercloud. It starts when wind inside the cloud starts to spin very quickly. A twisty tornado speeds across the ground, sucking up everything in its way.

Storm chasers observing a tornado in Kansas, USA

Amazing! **Some people track tornadoes for fun. They drive as close to the twister as they dare, then take video films and photographs. It's a very dangerous hobby!**

A tornado leaving a trail of damage

Is it true?

Tornadoes can pick up trains.

YES. In 1931, a tornado in Minnesota, USA, picked a train right off its tracks and dumped it in a ditch. Tornadoes often pick up cars and cows!

How quickly do tornadoes travel?

Most tornadoes travel at about 30 kph, but some are much speedier movers. They race along the ground as quickly as a car. What's more, the wind inside a tornado can blow at an amazing 480 kph.

Do tornadoes happen at sea?

Yes, they're called waterspouts. These giant twists of water can be over 1.5 kilometres tall. In the past, sailors thought waterspouts were sea monsters!

Waterspouts suck up tonnes of water from the sea

Firefighting plane

How do wildfires start?

They destroy huge patches of forest, and spread very quickly, especially in dry weather. Lightning starts hundreds of wildfires a year. But most fires are started intentionally by people to clear space for farms and fields. These fires can quickly get out of control.

Is it true?

Some trees have fireproof bark.

YES. Many trees die in forest fires because their wood easily catches fire. But some trees have special bark which protects the wood inside from the flames.

How do people fight wildfires?

Fighting a wildfire is difficult and dangerous. Special planes fly overhead spraying the forest with millions of litres of water. Firefighters on the ground try to hold back the fire with water and beaters.

Firefighters battle a large wildfire

What is a heatwave?

A heatwave is very hot weather which lasts much longer than usual. The scorching heat can kill people, animals and crops. It also dries up reservoirs, and melts the surface of roads.

Duststorm during the Midwest USA heatwave, 1937

Amazing! It can take hundreds of years for a forest to grow again after a fire. But sometimes fires can be good for forests. They clear space for new plants to grow.

Landslide

What makes the land slide?

A landslide is a huge fall of soil or mud which suddenly breaks off a cliff or mountainside and slides downhill. Some landslides are caused by volcanoes, heavy rain, or earthquakes, which make the ground shake and slip.

Where was the worst mudslide?

The worst mudslide happened in Colombia in South America. In 1985, a volcano erupted and melted masses of snow and ice, turning the soil to mud. The mud poured downhill at top speed and buried a whole town.

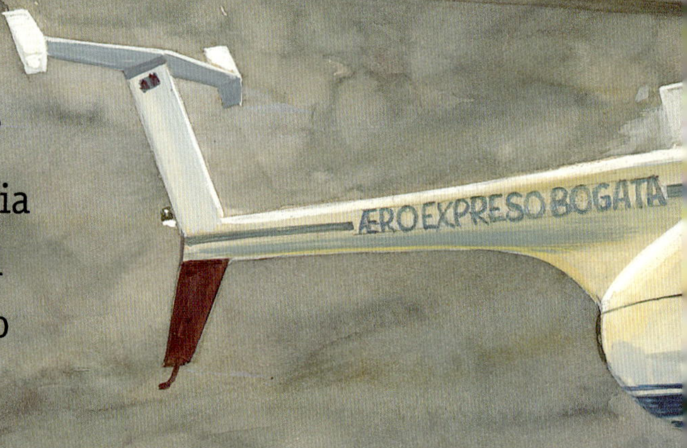

Mudslide survivors are rescued by helicopter in Armero, Colombia

Is it true?

Cutting down trees causes landslides.

YES. Tree roots are useful for sticking the soil together. If the trees are cut down, the soil turns to mud and washes away when it rains.

Why do cliffs collapse?

As the waves crash against a cliff, they wear the bottom of the cliff away. If the cliff becomes too top-heavy, it collapses into the sea. Along the east coast of England, whole cliff-top villages have toppled into the sea.

Cliff collapsing into the sea

Amazing! Mudslides can slide at high speeds of up to 110 kph. They can slither along for as much as 100 kilometres before coming to a stop.

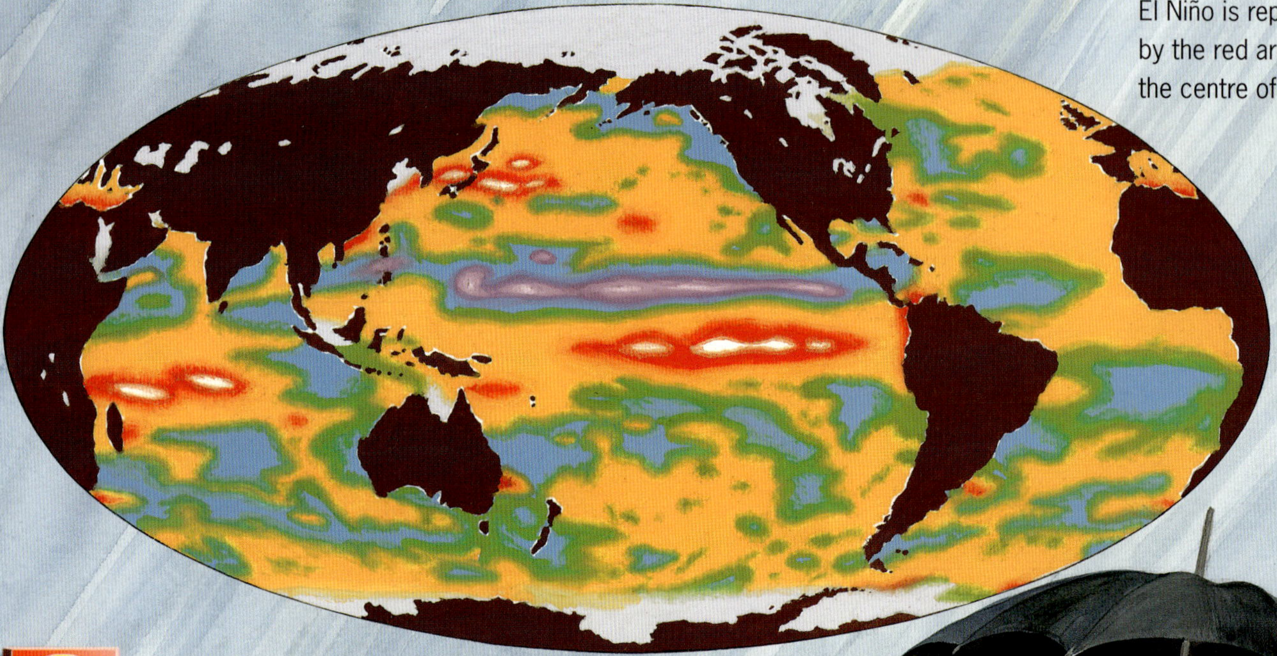

El Niño is represented by the red areas along the centre of the Earth

What is El Niño?

El Niño is a warm band of water which flows in the sea along the coast of South America. Scientists blame El Niño for changing the weather, by causing more storms, floods, droughts and tornadoes every few years.

Is it true?

It can rain cats and dogs.

NO. But you can get showers of fish, frogs, flowers, coal, nuts and even maggots! Scientists think the wind scoops them up, then they fall again in the rain.

What are monsoons?

Monsoons are winds which bring heavy rain to tropical places such as India and South East Asia, during the summer months. Farmers rely on this rain to water their crops, because during the cooler months, there might be little or no rainfall.

Amazing! A turtle once fell in a hailstone in the USA. It had somehow been sucked up into a thundercloud and covered in layers of ice.

The monsoon season can bring severe flooding

What is a sandstorm?

A sandstorm is a thick, choking cloud of sand whipped up by the wind in the desert. If you get caught in a sandstorm the best thing to do is cover your nose and mouth. Then you won't breathe the choking sand in.

Sandstorm in Africa

CHAPTER EIGHT

OUR EARTH

Earth seen from space

Is Earth a healthy planet?

Look at Earth from space and you see a mainly blue, watery planet with swirling white clouds. All looks well, but get closer, and you see a different picture. Parts of Earth are unhealthy – and all because of the way we live.

Does Earth need looking after?

Earth is our only home – we can't live on other planets. We need to look after it to make sure it stays a beautiful, healthy place. If we don't care for the Earth now, we will spoil it for the people of the future.

Can I help care for the Earth?

There are many things you can do in your everyday life to care for the Earth. This book tells you about some of them. Just think, if everyone did the same as you, Earth would be a better place to live.

Our Solar System has eight planets which orbit the Sun.

Is it true?
There is no other planet like Earth.

YES. There is only one Earth. It is special – it is the only planet known to have life on it. Perhaps one day life will be found on another planet, too.

Amazing! There has been life on Earth for approximately 3.5 billion years.

Is Earth's climate changing?

Earth's climate is slowly getting warmer. Scientists who study the climate have found that it is a little warmer now than it was 100 years ago. You may not notice the difference, but plants and animals do.

Climate study in the Antarctic

Is it true?

Trees reduce carbon dioxide in the atmosphere.

YES. Tree leaves take harmful carbon dioxide from the atmosphere and give out oxygen. We breathe the oxygen they make.

Cars and factories burn 'fossil fuels' which produce harmful 'greenhouse gases'

Why is the temperature rising?

It's getting warmer because of what the Earth's 7 billion people are doing. Because of the way we lead our lives, we are changing the Earth's climate. We are making the planet grow warmer.

Amazing! There is far more carbon dioxide in the atmosphere than there was 200 years ago. This is mainly why it's warmer today than it was in the past.

How are we making the temperature rise?

By burning 'fossil fuels' – coal, oil and natural gas – we are putting 'greenhouse gases', such as carbon dioxide, into the atmosphere. The gases surround the Earth and keep heat in.

What will happen as the temperature rises?

As the Earth's climate warms up, glaciers and the ice at the North and South Poles will melt, causing the sea level to rise. This will bring floods, and some islands will disappear. Deserts will spread, and droughts will occur.

Amazing! Cows are making the temperature rise. The smelly greenhouse gas methane comes from animals, such as cows, and from factories. Humans make it, too!

How can governments reduce carbon dioxide levels?

Burning petrol in cars puts carbon dioxide into the atmosphere. Governments can build transport systems that don't make carbon dioxide, and order more trees to be planted.

Electric railway

What can I do to help?

Use less electricity. This is because most electricity comes from burning fossil fuels which makes carbon dioxide. Switch off lights, TVs and computers when not in use.

Is it true?

If the Antarctic ice sheet melted, the sea level would rise.

YES. It holds two-thirds of the Earth's fresh water. If it melted, the sea would rise by up to 70 metres. Coastlines would change all over the world.

Antarctica

What other problems are caused by burning fossil fuels?

Sulphur dioxide is another harmful gas that comes from power stations and vehicles. It is very acidic, which means it eats things away. In the atmosphere, it mixes with droplets of moisture to make acid rain. Trees die when acid rain falls on them and on their soil.

Is it true?

Some polystyrene burger cartons are bad for the Earth's atmosphere.

YES. Some of them are bad because they're made using chemicals that damage the ozone layer. Many cartons are now made without these harmful chemicals.

Scandinavian forest damaged by acid rain

Is Earth's atmosphere being harmed?

There is a layer of helpful gas around the Earth called ozone. It protects us from the Sun's dangerous ultraviolet rays. Unfortunately, the ozone layer is damaged because humans have put harmful chemicals into the atmosphere.

Amazing!

When a nuclear power station at Chernobyl, Ukraine, exploded in 1986, radioactive material was sent into the atmosphere. Animals across Europe were contaminated by the radiation.

WARNING!

Always use a sunscreen in sunny weather to protect your skin from the Sun's rays.

Is nuclear power dangerous?

Nuclear power stations do not burn fossil fuels. Therefore, they do not make harmful gases. But they do make radioactive waste material. It is dangerous and will have to be guarded for many years into the future.

Underground storage of nuclear waste

Are there alternatives to fossil fuels?

There are other ways to make power. Solar panels collect energy from the Sun. The spinning propellers of wind turbines collect energy from the wind. Each of these energy-collectors makes electricity.

Amazing! Cars can be powered by all sorts of things – solar power, gas and even chicken droppings!

Wind turbines convert energy from the wind into electricity

Are there any other types of natural fuel?

In many countries small amounts of energy come from rotting plants and animal dung. The methane they give off is burned to provide light and heat. This type of fuel is called bio-gas.

Bio-gas plant in India

Are these fuels better for the Earth?

Yes, they are. Solar power, wind power and bio-gas are cleaner, or 'green', forms of energy. They don't make harmful gases. They don't pollute the atmosphere. They don't make acid rain. They don't harm the ozone layer.

Hoover Dam, USA

Is it true?

Electricity can be made from water.

YES. Running water is used to make electricity. This is hydroelectric power. The electricity is made by power stations built in or near dams.

Are animals in danger?

Thousands of different animals live on Earth. It is their planet, as well as ours. Sadly, because of what we do, many animals are in danger. An oil spill at sea harms seals, birds and fish. When forests are cut down, many animals lose their homes.

How many kinds of animals are in danger?

There are many thousands of different kinds of animals in danger. Some are so rare they are endangered. This means they are almost extinct – they have almost died out. If that happens, they will have gone forever.

What is being done to save animals?

Many endangered animals are now protected by law. It is wrong for people to harm them, or the places where they live. Some endangered animals are bred in zoos. This helps to increase their numbers.

Golden lion tamarin

Is it true?

Humans are causing animals to die out.

YES. It's said that one kind of animal dies out every 30 minutes because of what we're doing to the planet.

Cormorant covered in oil

Amazing!

Passenger pigeons used to form flocks of millions of birds, but they were hunted to extinction in the wild. The very last one, named Martha, died in 1914.

Why do people kill certain animals?

Animals are killed for lots of reasons. Birds are killed for their colourful feathers. Elephants are hunted for their ivory. Tigers are killed for their skins. It's against the law, but it still goes on.

Stuffed animals

Collecting rainforest plants

Amazing! Every year around 100 million animals and plants are taken without permission from the wild. It is because of this that they are endangered.

What about plants?

Like animals, plants can die out too. More than 30,000 different kinds of plants are in danger all over the world. Collectors take them from the wild, or pay local people to do it for them.

Is it true?

Sea turtles are hunted for their shells.

YES. Even though it's illegal, sea turtle shell, called tortoiseshell, is still used to make spectacle frames and souvenirs for tourists.

Illegal animal goods

What can I do to help?

Don't buy goods made from ivory, fur, coral or tortoiseshell. Don't pick or dig up wild plants. If you eat tuna fish, make sure it's dolphin-friendly. Dolphins die in some fishing nets.

Rainforest

Why are forests good for the Earth?

Forests are the 'lungs' of the planet. Their trees make much of the oxygen we breathe. Forests provide us with food and timber. Some medicines are made from plants found only in forests.

Are forests in danger?

Forests are in danger in many parts of the world. In some countries trees are killed by acid rain. Elsewhere, whole forests are cut down for their timber, or to make way for farm land.

Logger truck

What is being done to save forests?

Some governments have stopped cutting down the forests on their land. Many forests that are left are protected by law. Also, new forests are being planted, to grow timber like any other crop. It is grown to be cut down.

Amazing! Since 1980, an area of tropical forest six times the size of France has been turned into farm land, or plantations of oil palm, rubber and other crops.

Is it true?
Soil erosion can be seen from space.

YES. Trees keep soil in place. Where forests are cleared the soil wears away, or erodes, until only rock is left.

Soil erosion on Madagascar, seen from space

How much rubbish do people make?

Too much! People make rubbish and every household makes lots of it every day. In Britain, every family makes about 1.75 kilograms of rubbish each day. Over one year that adds up to more than half a tonne of rubbish!

Is it true?

Some rubbish is dumped at sea.

YES. **Every day thousands of tonnes of rubbish are thrown into the sea. The seabed is littered with rubbish, such as bits of plastic, that never rot away.**

Rubbish dump

Rubbish dumped at sea

What happens to all this rubbish?

Because so much rubbish is made, it's a problem to deal with it all. Some is burned inside furnaces. A lot is buried on the land. Some rubbish is collected and sent for recycling.

Burning rubbish in a furnace

Amazing!

The world's rubbish mountain grows by about 2 million tonnes every day.

What can I do to make less rubbish?

Put the three Rs into practice: Reduce, Reuse, Recycle. Reduce means use less of something. Reuse means use something again. Recycle is to save something so it can be made into a new thing.

What can I do with glass?

When glass bottles and jars are empty, wash them out and take them to a bottle bank. Most supermarkets have them. When they are full, the glass is taken to a factory where it is crushed, melted and made into new bottles and jars.

Amazing! Around 6 billion glass bottles and jars are used in Britain every year, but only three out of every ten are recycled.

What can I do with plastic?

Some kinds of plastic can be recycled. Plastic bottles for fizzy drinks are often made of recyclable plastic. It can be turned into material to make plastic parts for cars. These bottles can also be reused, by being made into useful items.

Reused plastic bottles

Paper recycling

What can I do with paper?

Most paper can be recycled, from newspapers and telephone directories to sweet wrappers and envelopes. It is made into new paper and cardboard.

Is it true?

Glass can be recycled over and over again.

YES. You just keep on crushing it, melting it and making it into new bottles and jars.

What can I do with aluminium cans?

Cans and tins that hold fizzy drinks and even sardines are often made from a lightweight metal called aluminium. Look for the ALU symbol on them. They can be melted down and made into new cans.

Amazing! In Britain we throw away around 11 million aluminium cans every day. If you think that's a lot, the USA throws out 200 million!

Reusing clothes

Can recycling

Using magnets to test cans

What can I do with steel cans?

Most food cans are made from steel. A magnet will stick to a steel can. If it doesn't stick, the can is probably made from aluminium. Wash the cans out and take them to a can bank. Steel is the world's most recycled material.

Is it true?

Christmas trees can be recycled.

YES. Real Christmas trees (not plastic ones!) can be cut into tiny pieces, called chippings, which are used by gardeners.

What can I do with old clothes?

Give old clothes to charity shops. They are sorted out and many are sold as second-hand clothes. Some old clothes are sent abroad. Tatty clothes are sent to textile mills where they are ripped to pieces and used to make felt.

What can I do with kitchen and garden waste?

Vegetable peelings, tea leaves and grass cuttings are 'green' waste. If you pile them into a heap in the garden, they will rot down to make compost.

Even some kinds of paper can be turned into compost

Why is compost good for the environment?

Compost is food for the soil. It contains nutrients (foods) which keep soil healthy. Using home-made compost means less peat compost is dug up from natural places, and animals' homes are saved.

Gardening with compost

Are there other ways of recycling green waste?

You don't need a garden to recycle green waste! You can make small amounts of compost and plant food inside a wormery – a container where a colony of worms live. Worm bins can be kept inside or outside.

Is it true?

Leaves make good compost.

YES. Leaves rot down slowly to become leaf mould. Put them in a black bag or an open-topped wire cage. After two years you'll have compost.

Amazing! Green waste in a rubbish tip makes dangerous methane gas, and liquid that can pollute water and kill wildlife. It's safer to make it into compost.

Polluted river

Are there any dangers to our food?

Some people are worried about genetically modified (GM) foods, where the genes – instructions – have been changed by scientists. Because this has not happened in nature, no one knows how safe these foods are.

Spraying crops with chemicals can harm the delicate balance of nature

Amazing! Pollen from crops that have had their genes changed can mix with organically grown crops. When this happens, an organic crop is no longer organic.

What does 'organic farming' mean?

It's a natural way of farming where crops are grown and animals raised without using man-made chemicals. Also, the plants and animals have not been changed in any way.

Organic farm of the past

Is it true?

GM crops need fewer pesticides.

YES. Scientists are changing the genes inside some crops so that they can resist diseases and pests on their own.

What can I do about it?

It's easy, and fun, to grow some foods at home, such as cress and tomatoes. Be organic, so don't put any chemicals on them. They'll taste good!

Tomato growing

What can I do at home?

Inside the house, start your own recycling centre, collecting materials that can be recycled. Reuse carrier bags, switch off electrical items when they're not in use, and don't leave taps dripping. Outside, get composting, and grow your own organic vegetables.

Amazing!

Even an alien would think Earth needs caring for. That's because there are 100,000 pieces of space junk whizzing around the planet.

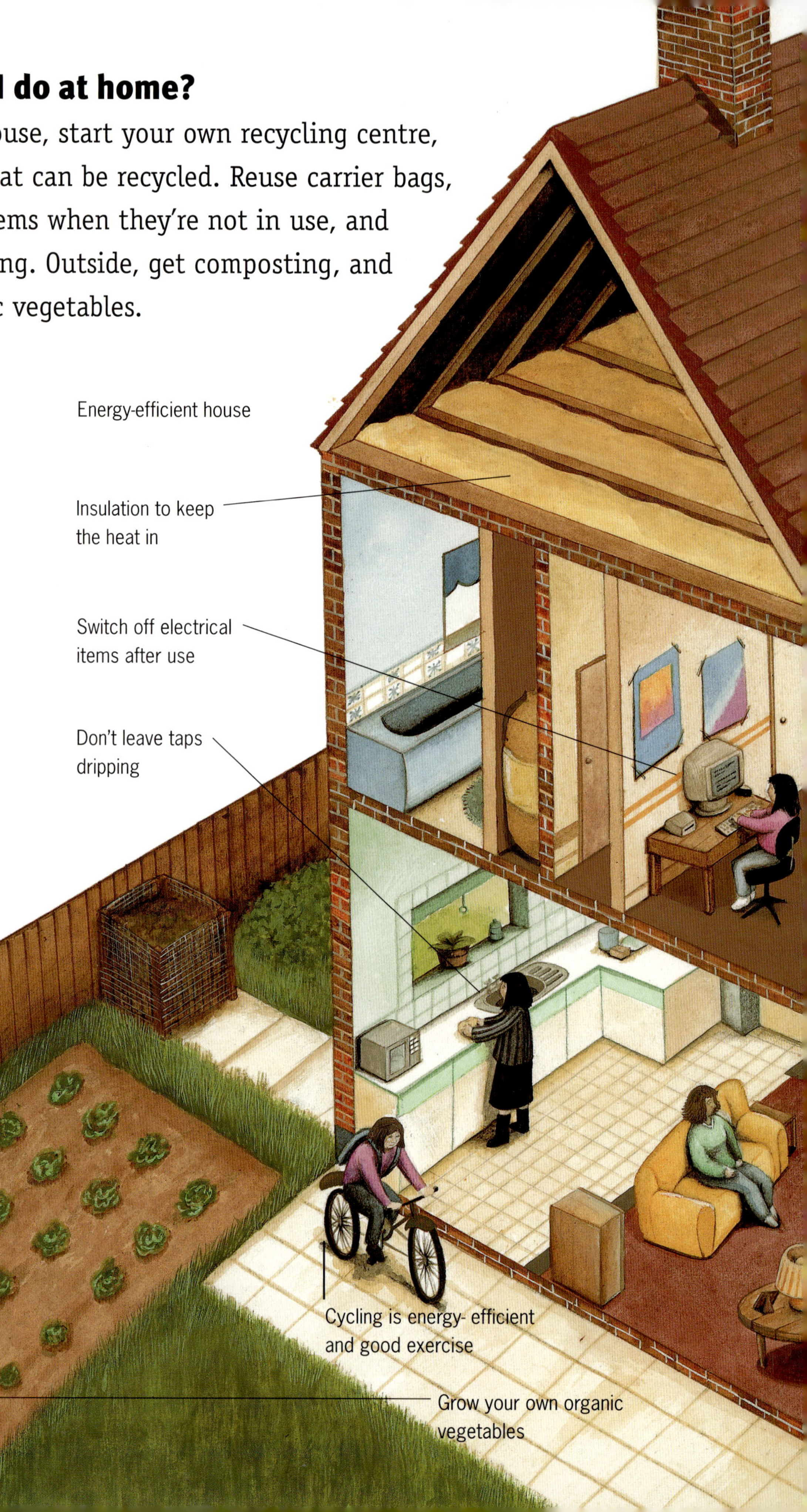

What can I do at school?

If your school has a Green Club, join it. If it doesn't, ask if one can be started. As at home, switch off lights when they're not in use, and collect paper, cans and glass for recycling. Walk or cycle to school. Try to use cars less.

Sorting rubbish for recycling

Is it true?

You can make a difference.

YES. Imagine if everyone in your class, your street, even your town recycled things. What a difference that would make!

How can I find out more?

If you would like to help make the Earth a better, safer place to live, now and in the future, you might like to join groups such as Greenpeace, Friends of the Earth or World Wide Fund for Nature. Your library will have their addresses.

Glossary

Acid rain Rain that contains chemicals which are harmful to nature.

Active A volcano that is still erupting.

Algae Tiny plants that live in water.

Amber Once liquid tree resin (sap) which has been fossilized.

Amphibian An animal that lives on land and in water, such as a frog.

Asteroid A small rocky body which orbits the Sun.

Astrology Using patterns in the sky as a guide to daily life.

Astronaut Someone who travels into space. The word means 'sailor of the stars'.

Astronomy The science of space-watching.

Atmosphere The gases or air surrounding a planet.

Axis The imaginary line around which a planet spins.

Bacteria Tiny, living things that live in soil, water and the air.

Bark The tough protective outer layer of a tree, which covers and protects the trunk and the roots.

Big Bang The huge explosion that created the Universe around 15 billion years ago.

Black hole A place in space with such strong gravity that not even light can escape from it.

Blizzard A winter storm with strong winds and heavy snow.

Butte A small, flat-topped hill in the desert.

Capsule A small spacecraft with room for one or two crew.

Carnivore An animal that eats only meat.

Climate The weather conditions in a particular place on Earth.

Comet A body of ice and rock with a long glowing tail that orbits the Sun.

Coniferous Trees which have needle-like leaves and cones, such as cedar, fir and spruce trees.

Constellation The pattern that stars seem to make in the sky, from our viewpoint on Earth.

Core The middle of something.

Cosmology The science of how the Universe (or 'cosmos') works.

Cosmonaut A Russian or Soviet astronaut. The word means 'sailor of the Universe'.

Crust The solid layer of rock on the surface of the Earth. It is about 8 km thick under the sea, and 40 km thick under the continents.

Cumulonimbus Another name for a tall, dark thundercloud.

Cynodont A type of reptile with fur, which evolved into mammals.

Dam A barrier built across a river to stop it flooding or to collect water in a reservoir.

Data Information.

Delta The end of a river where it flows into the sea.

Dinosaur A type of reptile that once lived on Earth, but which has died out.

Dormant A sleeping volcano that could erupt at any time.

Drought A time of very dry weather when less rain than normal falls.

Eclipse When light from the Sun or Moon is blocked out. A solar eclipse is when the Moon passes between the Earth and Sun, casting a shadow on the Earth. A lunar eclipse is when Earth passes between the Moon and Sun.

Equator The imaginary line which runs around the middle of the Earth.

Extinct A volcano that has stopped erupting.

Fault A crack in the Earth's crust.

Fold mountain A mountain made when one piece of the Earth's crust crashed into another and pushes up the land in between.

Fossil The remains of an ancient animal or plant preserved in rock.

Fossil fuels Fuels such as coal, oil and gas, made from fossilized remains.

Freshwater Water that does not taste salty. Rivers and many lakes are freshwater.

Galaxy A family of star systems that are held together by gravity. Our Solar System is in the Milky Way galaxy.

Genes The instructions that make living things what they are.

Greenhouse gas Gases, such as carbon dioxide or methane, which surround the Earth and keep heat in.

Habitat The surroundings in which an animal or plant lives.

Herbivore An animal that eats only plants.

Lava What magma is called when it erupts from a volcano.

Lens A curved piece of glass.

Lightning conductor A rod on the roof of a tall building which is attached to a strip of metal. It carries electricity from the lightning safely down to the ground.

Magma Rock deep beneath the Earth. It is so hot that it has melted.

Mammal An animal with a backbone that feeds its young on mother's milk.

Mantle The part of the Earth between its crust and its central core.

Meander A large bend in a river. Sometimes a meander gets cut off and forms an oxbow lake.

Mesa A large, flat-topped hill in the desert.

Meteorite A space rock that hits the Earth.

Meteoroid A small lump of space rock.

Missile A weapon that is thrown through the air.

Module A section of a space station.

Moon An object in space orbiting a planet.

Nebula A huge cloud of gas and dust where new stars are born.

Nuclear power Power made from radioactive material.

Nutrients Chemicals dissolved in water, used by plants in order to grow.

Observatory A place that houses telescopes and other instruments for viewing the sky.

Omnivore An animal that eats both meat and plants.

Orbit To travel around.

Organic A living thing, or something made from a living thing.

Oxygen A gas that animals breathe in and which keeps them alive.

Payload The cargo that a rocket carries into space.

Peat A dark brown material made from rotten plants.

Planet A body of gas or rock orbiting a star. Planets are not massive enough to be stars. They shine because they reflect the light of the star they are orbiting.

Poles The points at either end of a planet's axis, known as the north and south poles.

Prehistoric An ancient time before writing was invented.

Prey An animal which is killed by another animal for food.

Pulsar A small, dense, fast-spinning neutron star that gives out regular pulses of light and radio waves.

Quasar A region of space giving off more energy than almost any other.

Radioactive A substance that gives off harmful rays and particles.

Reservoirs Lakes used for storing water.

Seasons Different times of the year, when Earth's weather and life change according to the position of the Sun in the sky.

Soil erosion Wearing away of the soil.

Solar panels Mirrors that capture energy from the Sun and turn it into electricity.

Solar power Power made from the Sun.

Solar System Our Sun and everything that travels around it.

Stage A section of a rocket. Rockets usually have three stages.

Stalactite A spike made of stone which grows downwards from the ceiling of a cave.

Stalagmite A spike made of stone which grows upwards from the floor of a cave.

Star A huge ball of super-hot burning gas.

Submersible An underwater vehicle like a small submarine.

Tarn A small mountain lake carved out by ice millions of years ago.

Telescope An instrument that makes distant objects seem bigger and nearer. They collect light, radio waves, X-rays or other waves.

Twister Another name for a tornado.

Ultraviolet rays Harmful rays from the Sun.

Universe Everything that exists.

Vacuum An empty space with no air.

Wormhole A shortcut between two different parts of space.

Index

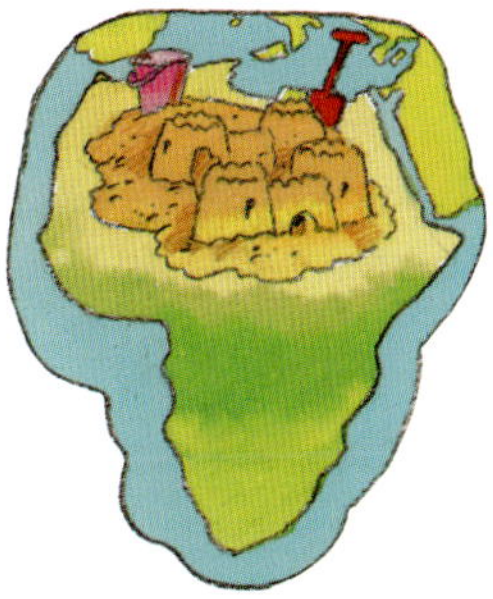